EMERSON
*and*
THE DREAM
*of*
AMERICA

I feel a new heart beating
with the love of the new beauty.
I am ready to die
out of nature, and be born
again into this new yet
unapproachable America . . .

Ralph Waldo Emerson
"Experience"

# EMERSON
## AND THE DREAM OF
# AMERICA

Finding Our Way
to a New and
Exceptional Age

Richard G. Geldard

Larson Publications
Burdett, New York

ISBN-10: 1-936012-46-6
ISBN-13: 978-1-936012-46-4
Library of Congress Control Number: 2010921167

Publisher's Cataloging-In-Publication Data
(Prepared by The Donohue Group, Inc.)

Geldard, Richard G., 1935-

   Emerson and the dream of America : finding our way to a new and exceptional age / Richard G. Geldard.

   p. : ill. ; cm.

   Includes bibliographical references and index.

   ISBN: 978-1-936012-46-6

1. Idealism, American. 2. Emerson, Ralph Waldo, 1803-1882--Political and social views. 3. Idealism--Social aspects--United States. 4. National characteristics, American. I. Title.

E169.1 .G45 2010
973/.01                                          2010921167

Published by Larson Publications
4936 NYS Route 414
Burdett, New York 14818 USA

larsonpublications.com

19 8 17 16 15 14 13 12 11 10

10 9 8 7 6 5 4 3 2 1

**Mixed Sources**
Product group from well-managed forests and other controlled sources
www.fsc.org Cert no. SW-COC-002283
© 1996 Forest Stewardship Council
FSC

# Contents

For Bob and Annie

# Preface

Wโดยที่ HEN Ralph Waldo Emerson set out to write a book entitled *Representative Men,* he chose as topics the philosopher, the mystic, the skeptic, the poet, the man of the world, and the writer. Oddly, he chose the great German scholar Johann Wolfgang von Goethe as his representative writer. With all the great writers of the world to choose from, his selection of Goethe broke the pattern of expectation. The others—Plato, Swedenborg, Montaigne, Shakespeare, and Napoleon—suited their categories easily enough, but not Goethe, until we read in the essay this sentence about the writer: *"In his eyes, a man is the faculty of reporting, and the universe is the possibility of being reported."* This was certainly Goethe, just as it became Emerson.

The seer of Concord was foremost a writer. He was also a philosopher, a poet, a mystic, something of a skeptic, at least of his own culture, and he has become a man of the world. As the sentence attests, he was indeed "the faculty of reporting" and as a well-traveled lecturer for over thirty years he saw his growing America as "the possibility of being reported."

The American composer Charles Ives, whose *Concord* sonata celebrates the central figures of New England Transcendentalism, made this assessment of Emerson's importance:

Though a great poet and prophet, he is greater, possibly, as an invader of the unknown—America's deepest explorer of the spiritual immensities, —a seer painting his discoveries in masses and with any color that may lie at hand—cosmic, religious, human, even sensuous; a recorder, freely describing the inevitable struggle in the soul's uprise—perceiving from this inward source alone, that every "ultimate fact is only the first of a new series."

Ideally, this is what a writer does. He or she represents the faculty of reporting as a fundamental way of being in the world and also must see the universe as available to the curious attention and investigation so crucial to important writing. The word "possibility" also attests to the limitless openness offered to the writer's mind by observation and experience. Nothing escapes.

Emerson began his writing career in *Nature* with this conviction: *"Undoubtedly we have no questions to ask which are unanswerable. We must trust the perfection of the creation so far, as to believe that whatever curiosity the order of things has awakened in our minds, the order of things can satisfy."*

No modest commentary such as this on Emerson's writing can substitute for personal reading of his own words. This endeavor contains many of those words, some perhaps unfamiliar to even those who consider themselves Emersonians. Hopefully, you the reader will be inspired to settle down in solitude with Emerson the writer, the reporter of what he was to name *"this new yet unapproachable America."*

As an admiring student of their work, I dedicate this book to a great American couple, Robert Richardson and Annie Dillard, both of whom represent the best of American writing. They are the faculty both of reporting the universe as possibility and of revealing an America worthy of our own best thoughts.

# Introduction

*E*MERSON *and the Dream of America* connects the life
and work of Ralph Waldo Emerson to the informing ideas
of America's founding. It hopes to show that Emerson was one of our
most important founding thinkers and that in contrast to the American
Dream, the Dream of America suggests something deeper, more fundamental to both individuals and the nation. It means a founding in which
the principles of life, liberty, and human dignity were to be enshrined
in law and carried out in practice, where fundamental human rights for
all, regardless of race or gender, would finally prevail. It means living
in dignity and freedom from oppression. And like our notion of the
American Dream it means opportunity, which for most people means
open doors, a path to fulfillment of hopes and dreams, and, simply, being
given a chance to succeed.

We know, of course, that the Dream of America had to overcome
its most severe challenge in the fact of slavery, our national nightmare,
which still troubles our sleep as well as our waking lives. That the tragedy
of an enslaved people on our shores still lives with us cannot be denied,
and that is why Emerson's words still have relevance and credibility.
Here, for example, is a passage from his 1862 speech "American Civilization," delivered in Washington, D.C., at the Smithsonian Institution:

The times put this question: Why cannot the best civilization be extended over the whole country, since the disorder of the less-civilized portion menaces the existence of the country? Is this secular progress we have described, this evolution of man to the highest powers, only to give him sensibility, and not to bring duties with it? Is he not to make his knowledge practical? to stand and to withstand? Is not civilization heroic also? Is it not for action? has it not a will? "There are periods," said Niebuhr, "when something much better than happiness and security of life is attainable." We live in a new and exceptionable age. America is another word for Opportunity. Our whole history appears like a last effort of the Divine Providence in behalf of the human race.

These times, too, put the same questions. It does not take much imagination to translate the Emerson of 1862 to the present circumstances of the nation. In fact, it was in 1985, a generation ago in America, that philosopher Stanley Cavell began a speech in New York with an observation clearly relevant to the America of today:

This is a most happy occasion for me and I do not wish to mar it by speaking of unhappy things. But I will not belittle it by using it to speak of anything less than what matters most to me as a teacher and a writer and a citizen. One of these matters I share in common with every thinking person on earth, the imagination, or the refusal of imagination, of nuclear war, the most famous issue now before the world. Another matter is, in comparison, one of the most obscure issues in the world, and I share it, at most, with a few other obscure persons, the inability of our American culture to listen to the words, to possess them in common, of one of the founding thinkers of our culture, Ralph Waldo Emerson, an inability which presents itself to me as our refusal to listen to ourselves, to our own best thoughts.

Then a professor at Harvard, Cavell already had done more than anyone to position Emerson as the founder of American philosophy. Now, more than two decades later, as the nation and world watch the first months and years of a new political era, we are witnessing a sea-change in the collective American mind. Although the election of Barack Obama can be seen as the singular event in this change, it can also be said that his election was the result of a fundamental change already in the wind. Whether or not this shift will truly catch the sails of real change is yet to be seen.

The plea to listen to Emerson comes at another crucial moment in the Dream of America. In the coming months and years, the issue of climate change and environmental reform will present our new leadership with its greatest challenge. Health care reform aside, it will be the issues of alternate energies and climate change, with America as the leader in preventing global catastrophe, that will spell success or failure for America and the planet.

It was Emerson in 1836, when he published *Nature*, who truly signaled a unique perspective for a new nation. Although Emerson's little book influenced very few people when it was first published in that year, it was the germ of an idea that began a process of changing the way Americans thought about the wilderness. Rather than thinking of untamed nature as "the Devil's playground," as the Puritans did, Emerson told us we could find God in His creation and that time spent alone in unspoiled nature could restore our spirits and bring us closer to the source of our being.

When Emerson's friend and disciple, Henry David Thoreau, moved into his cabin at Walden Pond, on a piece of Emerson's land, he began the process of putting into practice what Emerson was teaching. The movement grew, and it was in 1862—in the middle of the Civil War, and the same year that Thoreau died—that President Lincoln signed a bill that for the first time in all the world set aside a large tract of land to preserve it for all the people of America as wilderness forever. It was Yosemite Valley in California.

Less than a decade later, in 1871, Emerson and a group of friends traveled by train to San Francisco just two years after the final spike was driven in the newly completed tracks of the Continental Railroad. He went by coach and then horseback into Yosemite Valley. When he arrived there, the young John Muir, age thirty-three, heard that the great man was there and hastened to present himself, but he was so intimidated at the prospect of meeting the man who had so inspired him in his devotion to the natural world, that he could not bring himself to approach Emerson. Eventually, the next day, they met and a great friendship was established between the two naturalists.

Here is Muir's account of the occasion:

> When he came into the Valley I heard the hotel people saying with solemn emphasis, "Emerson is here." I was excited as I had never been excited before, and my heart throbbed as if an angel direct from heaven had alighted on the Sierran rocks. But so great was my awe and reverence, I did not dare to go to him or speak to him. I hovered on the outside of the crowd of people that were pressing forward to be introduced to him and shaking hands with him. Then I heard that in three or four days he was going away, and in the course of sheer desperation I wrote him a note and carried it to his hotel telling him that El Capitan and Tissiack demanded him to stay longer.

At the end of the visit with Muir, Emerson's party rode away from the Mariposa grove of great trees and Muir wrote of the moment: "Emerson lingered in the rear . . . and when he reached the top of the ridge, after all the rest of the party were over and out of sight, he turned his horse, took off his hat and waved me a last goodbye."

Emerson had the prescience to appreciate fully the unique character of the American enterprise as it hurtled westward, and to place himself in a position to speak directly to a wider and wider audience. For thirty years, roughly from 1835 to 1865, he lectured throughout America, except the deep South. Early on it was around the Eastern seaboard, but he ventured later in widening circles as the country expanded and small towns grew to cities.

Lecturing was the primary support for himself and his extended family. Despite all the inconveniences of travel in those years, he was basically on the road every year for six months. He spent the warmer months back home in Concord, preparing for the new lecture season.

Throughout his lectures and teaching, Emerson's primary subject was "the infinitude of the private man," a vision that spoke to the unlimited potential of the human mind in its progress through time. But attached to that potential was always the awareness of limitation in dealing with "the times," of taking action in the world at large. Then as now the question came down to two aspects of daily life: How shall we live and how do we solve the times?

Emerson was intelligent enough to know that the times seem perennially bad, especially as seen through the light-infused prism of an irrepressible idealism. More pragmatic individuals may see the times as an opportunity for personal advancement or, even more negatively, as reason for their personal failures. Passionate reformers respond to the times by advancing causes, offering programs, founding societies, holding conventions, writing books and articles, and making fervent speeches. Their ambition is to effect permanent change for the better, perhaps even to reform human nature in the process. At a minimum, they hope to improve the lives of the less fortunate and promote economic and social justice.

But the change Emerson sought, at least early in his career, comes only sporadically through these interventions. The times may improve through collective action and enlightened policies; but changing the collective mind of a large, dynamic, and diverse culture such as America's does not happen solely through political or social action. Genuine change is more profoundly rooted and is led by unique individuals with unique gifts employing less obvious means.

The title of this book hopes to make the connection between Emerson's vision and what the founders envisioned for the new republic they established. As Americans we are taught to think of our blessed country as the hope of the world. Ours is the grand experiment, a new horizon for humanity. In our recent history, with credibility diminished, moral standing suspect, we find ourselves anxious to find a new, revitalized place to stand among nations. With a new sense of possibility recently engendered, we dare to hope for genuine renewal. Ours is, given the magnitudes involved, a daunting task.

Emerson knew that being American meant living with a moral imperative. Living elsewhere, Switzerland, for example, where my wife was born, or Canada, say, there is no imperative to defend or fulfill a promise of some grand potential or sacred trust handed down to us by founders. In America, however, we have to live up to the Dream that promises to lead the world to equality, justice, and freedom. We are to be the gleaming city on the hill, destined to show what can take place when the restraints of ruling authority and oppression are thrown off to let the individual be free at last, free at last. America began to fulfill that promise (for a brief shining moment) from World War II through the social progress of the Sixties. But soon enough came Vietnam, Watergate, the glorification of greed, and now, since 9/11, the tragic adventurism in Iraq, and economic irresponsibility on a global scale.

America seemed to have lost its way and the great Dream was replaced by the Grim Reality of superpower geopolitical politics. The mood turned apocalyptic after 9/11 and the growing threat of nuclear proliferation. For a time, even a decade ago, the comments of Stanley Cavell in 1985, with his grave concern about the dangers of nuclear war, seemed overwrought and his wishful thinking that we might actually listen to the words of our Founding Thinker seemed, as he himself put it, too obscure. But now, Cavell's plea on both counts must be taken seriously.

In this book we listen to Emerson as he explains to us what he means by individual self-recovery and moral engagement with one's culture. We listen with the hope that hearing his inspired words will support the notion that fundamental change may indeed come now to America, and that his voice can be a powerful guide to personal and national self-recovery.

# 1
# Our Secret Melancholy

EMERSON began his essay "Experience" with the question, "Where do we find ourselves?" It is a question for the moment, not meant only for America in 1842 when he took pen to paper to answer. It seems painfully clear that at present America has entered a period of great change and uncertainty. Both of these perceptions cause deep anxiety.

Many of us, from time to time, have talked complacently about living uneasily in a deeply troubled world, in effect, living our ordinary lives in a state Emerson called a secret melancholy. In an orderly world, such thoughts are manageable, even philosophic in the stylish sense. Today, however, what was once a secret melancholy we find to be raw, open, and exposed. We can no longer afford to nurture, like the French, this little kernel of discontent like some kind of fashionable *ennui*.

Can Emerson, a nineteenth-century writer and lecturer known for his idealism and trenchant aphorisms, have something truly useful to say to us today? Are his words relevant to our personal and collective lives?

Emerson reminded us in "Fate" that we are incompetent to solve the times. It was a valid warning not to expect too much from programmatic solutions. Is it true that great engines like the "economy" run independently, irrespective of human intervention? In our most recent case, it is apparent that when human actions cause a crisis, human intervention must intervene to solve it. But Emerson also observed that "the times" usually move in natural cycles and in huge motions beyond human technology or correction. In such cases, we have to look inward to find a place to stand and a handle to grasp just to hold on during these careening rides.

There is an important difference between what Emerson called "the times" and what we call "the culture." In 1955, the critic Lionel Trilling, in the preface to a collection of literary essays entitled *The Opposing Self,* defined culture this way:

> I speak of the relation of the self to *culture* rather than to *society* because there is a useful ambiguity which attends the meaning of the word culture. It is the word by which we refer not only to a people's achieved work of intellect and imagination but also to its mere assumptions and unformulated valuations, to its habits, its manners, and its superstitions. The modern self is characterized by certain *powers of indignant perception* [italics mine] which, turned upon this unconscious portion of culture, have made it accessible to conscious thought.

Emerson was among this class of persons with powers of indignant perception. The word "indignant" here is key to understanding Emerson, in that he cannot be characterized as one who was *alienated* by his culture, or even *rebellious.* But he was *indignant* if by that word we understand what it is to be, in a genuine and not self-righteous way, morally offended. It is rejection in the face of perceived injustice and, for Emerson in particular, a culture of solely materialistic valuations. Further, Emerson's indignation allowed a series of perceptions which, as Trilling suggests, rendered unconscious portions of culture accessible to conscious thought.

Part of what Emerson meant by "self-culture" involves this elevation into conscious thought of what mostly remains hidden in the unconscious through inattention, habit, and conformity. We find it easier, even comforting, to allow the world to have its way with us, a tendency which includes the assumption that "the way things are" is normative. Self-culture begins in earnest when we consciously choose to question "the way things are" in favor of what is better, stronger, and more life-enhancing.

If we in our present culture are incompetent to solve the times, the question of what we *are* competent to do cries out for an answer. But the answer to cultural change should not need to be some skeptical derision of efforts at reform or, even worse, a cynical reaction to efforts to effect change. Emerson stakes his claim on a higher form of action, on solutions leading to a higher platform than most of us are accustomed to occupy.

Faced with the temptations of reform and activism (what Emerson called "association") he personally demurred, based on his own talents, but then he offered his solution. Here is a passage to hear from "New England Reformers."

> Men will live and communicate, and plough, and reap, and govern, as by added ethereal power, when once they are united; as in a celebrated experiment, by expiration and respiration exactly together, four persons lift a heavy man from the ground by the little finger only, and without sense of weight. But this union must be inward, and not one of covenants, and is to be reached by a reverse of the methods they use. The union is only perfect, when all the uniters are isolated. It is the union of friends who live in different streets or towns. Each man, if he attempts to join himself to others, is on all sides cramped and diminished of his proportion; and the stricter the union, the smaller and the more pitiful he is. But leave him alone, to recognize in every hour and place the secret soul, he will go up and down doing the works of a true member, and, to the astonishment of all, the work will be done with concert, though no man spoke. Government will be adamantine without any governor. The union must be ideal in actual individualism.

Here is the theme of the integrity of the mind, the unity of thought, feeling, and action within the individual applied in the world by that individual, who with others of similar unity then have the effect of concert. The objection to this line of reasoning is that the desired effect seems more likely to come magically rather than mechanically. Emerson, in fact, admits that, even dares to celebrate it. At the beginning of the above passage he says, "It is and will be magic." It is and will be a *metaphysical* movement and not a material one. And yet, the results will be tangible.

What Emerson means by unity and concert is that our actions, like our thoughts and our principles, can be applied broadly in the same spirit that brought about the self-recovery of our more personal spiritual seeking. It is in this way that "our own best thoughts" carry a societal significance beyond ordinary thinking. Our best thoughts, Emerson said, are actions in the world because consciousness is the ground of being and these thoughts make the world what it is.

This interpretation of spiritual action begs the question: Isn't this way of reacting to the state of crisis in America the same thing as saying, "Well, let's pray about it. Maybe God will put things right." The difference, of course, is that spiritual action of the Emersonian kind is not the same thing as praying for God as a transcendental agent to intervene on behalf of His people. As Emerson said in "Worship," "Men talk of mere morality, —which is much as if one should say, Poor God, with nobody to help him." Emersonian action asks us to find an effective course of action by bringing into harmony the faculties of mind, feeling, and firm moral principle. It then asks us to employ our talents, those nature-oriented resources within, to find the best expression for the need facing us. Only then will things change for the better.

The integrity of our own minds, he said, is the sacred place where action in the world has both its formulation and its final expression. This is the sacred space, the ground, of our own best thoughts. In a time like the present, when, as Yeats expressed it, "Things fall apart; the center cannot hold; / Mere anarchy is loosed upon the world," we must not look beyond our own resources to so-called divine intervention (The Second Coming?) or solely to some heroic human figure to step out of the shadows with a magical voice and brilliant solutions. The real work is with those who have the capacity to find concert among strangers working in unity toward a genuine transformation. It is, as Emerson expressed it, like lifting the heavy body of culture with little fingers working in concert.

We cannot pass from this topic without addressing the last sentence in the above passage. Emerson concludes his ecstatic plea for unity with "The union must be ideal in *actual* individualism." The word ideal here stands for consciousness at the ground of being, where Emerson's Over-Soul resides as the source of our own personal conscious life. Unless we grasp this principle and grant it credibility, we cannot claim genuine unity with the ground. All our so-called "thinking" without that ground is mere ego and self-interest. When Emerson uses the word "actual" to modify "individualism," he refers to that universal ground as the source of *actual* individuality. It is, as he has said in "Worship," ". . . that the last lesson of life, the choral song which rises from all elements and all angels, is, a voluntary obedience, a necessitated freedom."

The obedience to which he refers here is to that ground of being, and such obedience is qualitatively different from what orthodox religion means when it uses the phrase "the will of God." Connecting to a consciousness or intelligence greater than our personal thought mechanisms is the "voluntary obedience" in Emerson's idealism, and when the Harvard divines in 1840 were faced with this vision and sought to "save" Unitarianism from the Transcendental incursion, it was against this connection that they railed. By definition, most religious doctrines in their practice thrust apart the human from the divine, no matter how tenuously each dogma defines the separation. Transcendental idealism is the only spiritual philosophy evolved in the West that asserts an intimate and pervasive presence of a higher nature as part and parcel with the human. What the nature and substance of that presence may be, and how it exists and has meaning for us, remains the great mystery at the heart of the enterprise known as Spiritual Idealism.

Even without knowing the precise nature of this omnipresent and permeating consciousness, we know its opposite, what Emerson calls "inner death." When he speaks of "we" in this next passage, he is referring to American culture, which he then describes.

> We do not believe that any education, any system of philosophy, any influence of genius, will ever give depth of insight to a superficial mind. Having settled ourselves into this infidelity, our skill is expended to procure alleviations, diversion, opiates. We adorn the victim with manual skill, his tongue with languages, his body with inoffensive and comely manners. So have we cunningly hid the tragedy of limitation and inner death we cannot avert. Is it strange that society should be devoured by a secret melancholy, which breaks through all its smiles, and all its gayety [sic] and games?

The relevance of this description of our "tragedy of limitation" is frightening because it suggests a submission to a general condition we believe to be intractable. When Emerson began "Fate" with the observation, "Our America has a bad name for superficialness," he was doing more than merely stating what we already know. "Fate" is a strong example of Emerson's "powers of indignant perception," but it is also a plea for radical intervention. What was true in 1844 is certainly more so now. The difference is in the degree of this inner death, our secret melancholy, and the nature of the opiates we employ to remain in a condition of ignorance.

Rather than address this condition individually or collectively, we as a culture demur and give in to soothing alleviations, diversions, and opiates. The proliferation of electronic chatter alone is enough to stifle any instinct to rise above it to discover something more substantial. We know better, of course.

Emerson certainly maintained a positive conviction in the face of what seems to us as an intractable malaise. Consider, for example, this outburst further along in the essay:

Life must be lived on a higher plane. We must go up to a higher platform, to which we are always invited to ascend; there, the whole aspect of things changes. I resist the skepticism of our education, and of our educated men. I do not believe that the differences of opinion and character in men are organic. I do not recognize, beside the class of the good and the wise, a permanent class of skeptics, or a class of conservatives, or of malignants, or of materialists. I do not believe in two classes.

Since Emerson himself lived and wrote on this higher platform, why not join him? It will take muscular restraint to turn away from diversions and opiates, but the rewards are great enough and might actually save our lives. We might find that "The soul lets no man go without some visitations and holy days of a diviner presence." Is work involved? It was the kind but firm Spinoza who told us that anything truly excellent is hard and not easily achieved. There is a climb to a more rigorous language and the exactions of thought, but if we are reasonably confident of the rewards and of a more sublime view from the summit, then why not begin the climb? In "The Oversoul," Emerson declared, "God will not make himself manifest to cowards." The same could be said for making manifest the Dream of America.

The challenge of joining Emerson on this higher platform presents certain problems of beginning. My choice is to go back in time to the foundations of what we now call the Perennial Philosophy, that esoteric tradition sometimes linked with mysticism. It was for Emerson the basis of his idealism, as evidenced by his devotion to the Presocratics, Plato, Plotinus, and subsequently to Wordsworth, Coleridge, and the Greek scholar and translator Thomas Taylor.

# 2
# Deeper Prisons

IN "Self-Reliance" Emerson said, "There is a class of persons to whom by all spiritual affinity I am bought and sold; for them I will go to prison if need be." The literal prison here reflects his commitment to Idealism and the examined life. But as we shall see, metaphoric prisons in which we are confined were also legion in Emerson's mind.

Emerson had experience of the more literal confinement as a result of his duties as a young minister. During a visit to Ellen Emerson's home in Concord, New Hampshire, in 1828, he went into the local prison there. Later he wrote in his journal, "I visited the prison and went into the cells. At this season they shut up the convicts in these little granite chambers at about 4 o'clock *P.M. and let them out about 7 o'clock A.M.—15 dreadful hours.*"

But it is the psychic prisons, still echoing the literal one, that enter pointedly in "Intellect" as a form of psychological confinement, as when we lose mastery of the rampant activity of the untempered mind. As he confirmed from his own experience, "We have little control over our thoughts. We are the prisoners of ideas." This startling statement, so contrary to our notion of the friendly, even rewarding world of ideas, reveals as few others of his observations do, something of the radical Emerson. What, we ask, is so wrong with ideas?

Before we can fully grasp Emerson's meaning here, however, we have to sift through the various terms he used to describe mental activity. Ideas can arise from any of these faculties of mind, but not, in Emerson's sense of the word, from the higher intellect. This faculty is closest to what we understand by a higher faculty, or what in the Indian Vedic texts is called *buddhi*—discrimination.

First, Intellect for Emerson does not mean intellectual, in the sense that we have in America an "intellectual community." As Richard Hofstadter has told us, the intellectual is an alienated figure in American life, not generally trusted by the culture. This was never more true than in the first decade of this new century, when the political and religious leadership at the national level prided itself on its disdain of all things intellectual. It might also be said that those who are overtly anti-intellectual are also unaware of the intellect as a distinct mental faculty. Only in that sense can there said to be a relationship between the two terms.

Nor does Emerson's "intellect" mean intelligence, that varying quality of mental capacity shared by all living creatures and delineated in human beings by IQ test scores and the ability to function in society. Emerson would say that the (capitalized) Intellect functions just as well in an individual of limited intelligence as it will in one of greater. "Do you think the porter and the cook have no anecdotes, no experiences, no wonders for you?" he asks in "Intellect."

Rather than define Intellect through other terms, Emerson describes how this faculty operates: "Neither by detachment, neither by aggregation, is the integrity of the intellect transmitted to its works, but by a vigilance which brings the intellect in its greatness and best state to operate every moment." Intellect, then, manifests itself in the mind through intuitive insight, flowing into consciousness unbidden from within, particularly when the attention is focused "by a vigilance" upon some object, whether it be another person, something in nature, or a page of text. Intellect floats an image of truth before our inner sight and, if we are attentive, we "see."

Only later does the mind begin its constant play in the effort to bring the insight from the intuition to the understanding where ideas form. Emerson's strong recommendation at such moments is to shut down the ordinary flow of thought because it represents a claim, the ego's desire to grasp to itself something which might be profitable. An idea, then, describes an artifact in the mind in which we may become confined, darkly confined, where the rest of the world is literally out of sight while we formulate plans to capitalize on this new "thing." Ah, we claim in this unlit space, *my* idea.

It is in this context that Emerson cautions us throughout this essay that "Every thought is a prison," and that "every heaven is also a prison." A heaven is a prison because it takes us out of the living world into a space totally other, where we can no longer participate actively in our present existence with all of its contingencies. And in "Experience" we are reminded that "Temperament . . . shuts us in a prison of glass which we cannot see." This last image makes concrete the most challenging confinement because temperament represents who or what we are all day. It is our personality, the way we are constituted. To be confined to temperament will not allow progress in the formation of character, or what Emerson called self-recovery.

This journey through some of the attributes of mind still begs the question, What's so wrong with ideas? Ideas make money, they create programs, political and social systems, theories of art, science, economics, on and on. This application of a creative idea is not Emerson's target, however. He is after the kind of thought that stops us in our progress of self-recovery, in the sense of "having ideas" about a situation or condition. Such an idea can be thought of as rationalization, an attitude, an excuse, or just an artificial stopping point on the path, a place where, because we are tired or impatient, we find ourselves attracted by someone else's sales pitch or answer to a problem. It is, in fact, the difference between an idea as something that comes to mind as a plan or a design as opposed to a truth, or an insight into the center of universal principle. The former is an interruption, whereas the latter is a signpost in our journey.

Premature satisfactions are the realm of the quick answer, the slick formula on television from a popular guru or the book with five simple steps to Enlightenment. Such ideas can seduce us away from the real work of shedding false notions and beginning instead to pay close attention to the inner voice of Intellect. Ideas are the quick fix that brings relief to our existential malaise and metaphysical doubts.

The most attractive prison, one which seduces us as the comfort of bed does after a hard day, is repose. Here, central to "Intellect" is Emerson's explanation of "repose."

> God offers to every mind its choice between truth and repose. Take which you please, —you can never have both. Between these, as a pendulum, man oscillates. He in whom the love of repose predominates will accept the first creed, the first philosophy, the first political party he meets, —most likely his father's. He gets rest, commodity, and reputation; but he shuts the door of truth. He in whom the love of truth predominates will keep himself aloof from all moorings, and afloat. He will abstain from dogmatism, and recognize all the opposite negations, between which, as walls, his being is swung. He submits to the inconvenience of suspense and imperfect opinion, but he is a candidate for truth, as the other is not, and respects the highest law of his being.

This passage sets up the either/or choice of the examined life, and since Emerson chooses to use the word "truth" in opposition to repose we know where he stands. Here, in the pursuit of truth, is the home of "our best thoughts." But what of "repose"? Rest, commodity, and reputation seem just rewards of hard work. The assumption behind Emerson's choice of "rewards" is that the path of truth, being spiritual in nature, means living life "in the spirit," as Oliver Wendell Holmes described Emersonian Idealism. The dubious rewards, the passage adds, are the inconveniences of suspense and imperfect opinion. These, of course, represent our true condition. The opposite—certainty, security in opinions, not to mention comfort, commodity, and reputation—describe the incarcerations of repose, like the prisoner secure in the knowledge of his dinner.

Obviously, the opposite of incarceration is freedom, and it is Emerson's notion of Intellect that turns the key of the prison door. What this freedom looks and feels like appears like this in "Intellect."

> The growth of the intellect is spontaneous in every expansion. The mind that grows could not predict the times, the means, the mode of that spontaneity. God enters by a private door into every individual. Long prior to the age of reflection is the thinking of the mind. Out of darkness, it came insensibly into the marvelous light of to-day. In the period of infancy it accepted and disposed of all impressions from the surrounding creation after its own way.

Not surprisingly, freedom is characterized by spontaneity, expansion, growth, and light. When we apply those terms to the laws of the mind, we begin to acquire a real taste for psychological and spiritual freedom. Notions of assigning value, of good vs. evil are not involved. If as Hamlet said, nothing is good or bad but thinking makes it so, Intellect is the faculty we employ to move beyond polarized thinking into the neutral space where good and bad do not enter the picture. We recognize this neutral space when the observing "I" is in place, watching the movements in mind without judgment. When we are in this state, we see these fundamental principles: I am; the world is; God is. The proverbial devil is confined to the details.

None of this is possible unless Intellect takes charge of the turbulent mind and brings some degree of order into its operations. "What is life but what a man is thinking of all day?" Emerson's question should not surprise us, but we are scarcely aware of this simple fact, so habitual is the state of consciousness involved. When the master is not at home, the servants play, and one of their favorite games is Lord of the Manor.

When the imagination is master, the house turns into fantasy land. When the analyzing mind turns master, the house is a somber library devoted to classification and order. When the ego is in charge, the house turns into a power game of dominance and self-gratification. If Intellect stays away too long or, worse yet, is never in residence, the house falls into disarray, one room devoted to this, another to that. Fragmentation rules.

Emerson tells us that when the logical faculty takes charge instead of serving Intellect, it begins to create propositions, and then it is no longer serving the process of self-recovery. When the logical faculty takes charge, it is easily imprisoned by posing questions like this: The philosopher from Crete declares, "All Cretans are liars." Are we to believe him or not? Logic falls apart facing such a paradox. When the discursive mind takes charge, it tends to organize and plan and comment on everything that takes place in the house. It forms opinions, asserts control, moves furniture, and disrupts the kitchen. It won't leave well enough alone.

The last stage, and the most difficult, is conscious reflection.

At last comes the era of reflection, when we not only observe, but take pains to observe; when we of set purpose sit down to consider an abstract truth; when we keep the mind's eye open, whilst we converse, whilst we read, whilst we act, intent to learn the secret law of some class of facts.

Reflection is the most difficult of mental disciplines because it sounds as if it should be intentional; but the reality is that Intellect prefers to offer its insights unbidden, not controlled by a lesser faculty. We are reminded again that "the act of reflection takes place in the mind." Not being able to respond purely to its calling is, as Emerson told us earlier, the most unhandsome and troublesome part of our nature. "I would put myself in the attitude to look in the eye an abstract truth, and I cannot. I blench and withdraw on this side and on that. I seem to know what he meant who said, 'No man can see God face to face and live'." As the wise man said, "God comes to see us without bell," because the visitation of truth cannot be commanded. And yet, once the insight has come to mind, when we are prepared, reflection can be the means by which it forms into expression and becomes of use to us.

Emerson's great gift was wisdom transformed into art, his ability to find the form and then the eloquence to convey the subtle mysteries of a mind not confined to reductive constraints. Other geniuses reveal the secrets of nature or the heights and depths of human feeling or the mysteries of the universe, but Emerson's genius was drawn early on to the infinitude of the mind as it applied itself to ordinary life. And when he declared in "Self-Reliance" that "nothing is at last sacred but the integrity of your own mind," he nailed his thesis to the door of the religious establishment and began his reformation. But at the same time, he only set the stage for his life-long demonstration of what he regarded as a fundamental axiom.

# 3

# Emerson and American Religion

CENTRAL to the idea of the Dream of America is the way in which our people relate to the religious experience—to God, or their idea of God. In this respect Emerson's personal experience is not unique, although the impact and importance of that experience has been singularly crucial. The writer and critic Harold Bloom has gone so far as to say that Emerson is the father of the American religion. What that means is the story of this chapter.

If the Dream of America means that we as a people live together in tolerance and equality, respecting one another's values and dreams of the good life, then religious tolerance must be central to that ideal. Very few people would now say that we live in a religiously tolerant society. If, as polls suggest, 94 percent of Americans say they believe in God, then religious belief plays an important role in our relations with one another.

Emerson's Spiritual Idealism was founded on the principle of individual conscience and personal belief devoid of any external authority. As a student at Divinity College at Harvard, he came to that view partly because he was exposed to the latest scholarship from Germany, which firmly established the authorship and dating of the Old and New

Testaments. The effect of this scholarship severely reduced the authority of Holy Writ as divinely inspired and resulted in the religious crisis in America in the 1820s.

On the evening of July 15, 1838, at the invitation of the graduates of Divinity College, Emerson gave his now famous Divinity School Address (see Appendix II for excerpts from that address). In it, Emerson affirmed his now firmly established convictions that the person of Jesus had been altered by early Church fathers to deify him rather than present him as another great prophet and teacher of spiritual principles. As Emerson said in a key passage about the person of Jesus:

> He said, in this jubilee of sublime emotion, 'I am divine. Through me, God acts; through me, speaks. Would you see God, see me; or, see thee, when thou also thinkest as I now think.' But what a distortion did his doctrine and memory suffer in the same, in the next, and the following ages! There is no doctrine of the Reason which will bear to be taught by the Understanding. The understanding caught this high chant from the poet's lips, and said, in the next age, 'This was Jehovah come down out of heaven. I will kill you, if you say he was a man.'

This passage was enough to brand Emerson as a heretic, and as a result he was banned from speaking at Harvard for over thirty years. Two serious blasphemous statements from that passage were critical to condemnation by the Harvard faculty. The first was misquoting statements from the gospels, putting words in the mouth of Jesus that he never spoke. The second was questioning Christ's unique divinity. But Emerson held to these statements, saying that all persons contain the same divine spark within, which in turn explained and justified the so-called mis-quoting from scripture.

What is important for the argument here is that Emerson's remarks in this sermon make little or no mention of textual matters. He was not arguing from scripture but from an inner knowing or *gnosis*. There is no plea for textual authority or adherence to doctrine. Emerson was then and is still accused of playing fast and loose with God's Word in a number of places, but in this case his purpose always was to express his sense of the *meaning* of scripture. It is, in fact, a technique common to a number of Charismatic preachers today, who expand upon biblical text for their own ends. Indeed, an entire Bible, the Amplified, popular among the evangelical sects, can be said to do something quite similar. It blurs the line between translation and transliteration for the sole purpose of establishing "amplified" meaning.

In Fundamentalist churches, preachers seldom misquote or amplify the text. Their approach is to interpret given text in terms immediately applicable to people's lives with exactitude, assuming that the words apply directly to the given moment and are to be taken literally. It would diminish the impact of the reading to alter or amplify the text in any way.

In Emerson's time, his misquotes and other doctrinal liberties were treated as heresy by the assembled Fathers of Unitarian Harvard, most particularly Andrews Norton, Professor Emeritus of Divinity College and, from that July evening on, Norton was Emerson's adversary. What Emerson had done was to challenge his Unitarian brothers to acknowledge the spiritual dimension within religious practice and to take seriously the human need to apprehend and then begin to ground their lives in that dimension.

The charge of heresy was real enough. Even though the Unitarian movement had generally accepted the humanity of Jesus and separated itself from Trinitarian belief, Emerson's assertion that Jesus shared his consciousness of and connection to God with all human beings was a direct challenge to accepted belief in the uniqueness, if not unique divinity, of Jesus. Emerson's heresy was to assert that we too, as human beings, like Jesus himself, possess the same divine spark—that God is not totally "other" but is, rather, part and parcel of who we are. As Robert Richardson so clearly states the matter, where Emerson differed from doctrine "was in his conviction that Christianity was founded on human nature, not on the Bible. 'They call it Christianity,' Emerson said. 'I call it consciousness.'"

If the battle lines are to be drawn between biblical authority on one hand and consciousness on the other, especially if the sense of ordinary consciousness is one of the combatants, we have no contest. After all, consciousness as commonly understood refers to ordinary thinking—what Emerson meant when he said "what a man was thinking all day." But if by consciousness we (including Emerson) mean a higher consciousness capable of apprehending higher laws, which may include the Divine Presence, then a genuine debate is not only possible but necessary. We are reminded of Paul's assertion: "We have the mind of Christ."

The debate, if one is even possible, should take place between two distinct and arguable points of view. The first, American Fundamentalism, holds today that the only acceptable approach to Christian belief demands immovable allegiance to the inerrant, infallible, and divinely inspired Holy Bible. In effect, whatever the Bible says is so. Period. The second, and we shall call it Spiritual Idealism, holds that consciousness in human beings includes the faculty of Universal Consciousness that is attributable to Absolute Being and that this consciousness is accessible to human beings as both law and *gnosis*. This consciousness also leads to the ultimate truth of reality.

What I have called Spiritual Idealism was also a philosophical, religious, and literary movement of the early decades of the nineteenth century in Germany and England. The movement was in part a reaction to the excessive rationality of the preceding English Enlightenment and the skeptical philosophy of Hume and others. In the broadest sense, Spiritual Idealism was also part of the ancient stream of thought given the name Perennial Philosophy, which Emerson and the other Transcendentalists of New England were deeply influenced by and which they adapted to their own circumstances and culture. The works of Emerson and Thoreau, in particular, embody this point of view.

The crisis of faith within New England Christianity in the early decades of the nineteenth century was the result of these historical and intellectual forces filtering down to the ordinary church-goer through ministers torn between biblical authority and the so-called new think-ing. It was Emerson's struggle with these two positions that prompted his eventual resignation from the Church and was certainly prompted in part by the serious questions raised by the new German scholarship as represented by H.K. Graf, Julius Wellhausen, Johann Gottfried Eich-horn, and Johann Jakob Griesbach.

Throughout New England in this period, Sunday services were increasingly a confusion of theological struggles. Old time Puritans and Calvinists still preached fire and brimstone sermons warning of eternal damnation and God's arbitrary election, the doctrine that salvation or damnation was pre-determined. The liberal wing, given voice by William Ellery Channing and Henry Ware, Jr., preached a new dispensation, that human beings were given freedom of choice in this world and that the purpose of life on earth is to confront the hard choices and make the right ones: Human beings held the reins of their own salvation or damnation. The words of Jesus remained the arbiter of the moral life.

This crisis came to a head in the 1820s when Harvard College became the center of the liberal wing of Calvinism. The Unitarian Association was founded in 1825, effectively solidifying the liberal wing in east-ern Massachusetts, with Harvard as its intellectual center and training ground for new ministers. The effect of this struggle in broader terms was not only to reject the harsh determinism of the conservatives but to redefine literally what it meant to be a human being.

The influence of German Idealism can only have been marginal at best in this atmosphere because of the intellectual rigor it required. For the ordinary citizen, however, who may have instinctively rejected the harsh implications of Calvinist determinism, the new liberalism was certainly welcome. Going to church was no longer a fearful experience, a weekly occasion of being reminded that our fate was sealed in God's ledger and that eternal damnation loomed for most of us, with only a privileged handful predestined for paradise.

During his brief role as Junior Minister of the Second Church, Emer-son wrote sermons whose purpose was to reassure, uplift, and inspire.

He emphasized the importance of cultivating a *religious feeling* to sustain us, rather than focusing on conduct and good works. Daniel Howe's *The Unitarian Conscience* points out the strength of the new Unitarian influence during this period of crisis. Rather than argue freedom vs. determinism from the pulpit, the new Unitarians emphasized instead that the faculty we identify as conscience was an instrument capable of guiding our lives and was based on feeling rather than intellect.

An example of this approach to the hearts and minds of his parishioners is Emerson's strongest sermon, entitled "Pray without Ceasing," which he gave fourteen times in various pulpits from 1826 to 1828 and which was based on the text from Paul's letter to the Thessalonians (I Thes., 5:17). The text and Emerson's reading of the verse is a prime example of the conflict among competing views of biblical interpretation.

Paul's admonition to the brothers of the early Church in Thessalonika to "pray without ceasing" is commonly meant to be a fundamental directive of the religious life. The various prayers were prescribed and their meaning clear. Here are several verses from King James Version, chapter five:

> Now we exhort you, brethren, warn them that are unruly, comfort the feebleminded, support the weak, be patient toward all men.
>
> 15: See that none render evil for evil unto any man; but ever follow that which is good, both among yourselves, and to all men.
>
> 16: Rejoice evermore.
>
> 17: Pray without ceasing.
>
> 18: In every thing give thanks: for this is the will of God in Christ Jesus concerning you.

In this context the admonition to pray without ceasing either means "don't forget to pray often," or literally to pray all the time. For Emerson, this verse came to mind as a result of a chance remark from a farm laborer named Tarbox, who said to Emerson one day while they were working in the fields that men were always praying and that all prayers were answered.

Emerson's sermon on the verse reflected on the farmer's remark and brought to mind for the young minister that "every desire of the human mind, is a prayer uttered to God and registered in heaven." Therefore, we had better be careful what we pray for and we must be more conscious of the inner life and not just our actions in the world. True spiritual life, in other words, is interior, constant, real, and effective. So, when Emerson said later on that reality for a human being is what we think about all day, he was affirming the principle that religious faith is based on consciousness, not scripture. What we think, we are, and what the world is.

This kind of sermonizing was meant to instigate a shift in consciousness for the listener. The effect was (and is) to draw the attention inward, to see and then to understand what it really means to take part in life. It also suggested that the life of the mind (what we think) is more important than the life of the body (what we do). Eventually, the life of the mind, leading from seeing to understanding to knowledge, results in wisdom, the love of which is philosophy.

The crisis of faith in the New England of the 1820s manifested two radical positions: Puritan/Calvinist orthodoxy and Transcendentalism. Between them, for the majority, the pallid center limped along, content to support the new commercial and increasingly secular society. The conservative Puritan/Calvinist remnant would gradually move westward and later form the basis of Fundamentalism in America, based as it was on a mistrust of intellectual revisionism. The writings of the famous witch-hunting Cotton Mather, one hundred years earlier, embodied the central tenets of the Puritan devotion to biblical authority. In a tract entitled "What Must I Do to Be Saved?" Mather answers:

My Design is to bring in a Good and full Answer to this Weighty Question, Oh! how Thankful ought we to be, for the Glorious Gospel of the Blessed God, that makes us able to Answer it! The Gospel which we have in our hands, this a Gospel of such astonishing Mystery, of such Heavenly Majesty, and of such Consummate Purity, that it can be no other than the Word of God; It must be of a Divine Original. Oh! highly Favoured People, who know this Joyful Sound! Oh! Unavoidably and Inexcusably Wretched, if we disregard it.

Under the sway of his own eloquence, Mather laid the groundwork for the excesses of Fundamentalism to come two hundred years later— excesses which would blind many to the sometimes irrational devotion to scriptural authority, a devotion eventually damaging to the genuine spirit of the gospels. Reading Mather today prompts the reaction that he "doth protest too much," that he feared no doubt that the spirit of his grandfather's and father's era was fading before his eyes. Certainly, at the end of his life, with the infamous Salem witch trials behind him and executions on his conscience, he bitterly complained that he had been judged unfairly.

The great irony of Emerson's complaint of spiritual listlessness and empty preaching in his own time is that the exact same complaints brought about a spiritual awakening in America of a very different sort, one which currently manifests itself as Evangelical Christianity and its more extreme cousin, Fundamentalism. That these two strains of spiritual longing emerge indeed from the same source leads to misunderstanding and deep resentment, but also provides the means of looking at each strain with a less antagonistic eye.

Before Emerson and Transcendentalism, the Great Awakening of 1740–43 brought from England a new evangelical fervor to the landscape, one completely outside of the established churches. People gathered by the thousands in the open air and in tents to hear preachers like Britain's George Whitefield call for religious conversion and dedication to Christ, thus establishing the theme of born-again conversion which would become so important in the coming century. Itinerant preachers followed the westward expansion and established so-called tent ministries, prefiguring the crusades of Billy Graham. It is difficult to escape the conclusion that as the country moved away from the coastal towns into the interior, there emerged a compatible religious fervor among the pioneers. Here was religion that was not meant to be contained or civilized. Its main thrust was abandon.

America became particularly susceptible to evangelical movements because of the presence of the wilderness and the diversity of the population, the openness of religious choice, and the lack of firm grounding in religious tradition. At the time of the Revolution and the framing of the Constitution, religious freedom became central to the newly forming nation, making it certain that proselytizing among the various denominations would become the norm. If the church down the street had a charismatic preacher, people gathered there, and finding such a preacher became important business for budding denominations.

In terms of the later movement towards Fundamentalism, the Great Awakening was important because the evangelical movement drew the less educated, the less sophisticated into the orbit of religious doctrine and biblical interpretation, establishing a pattern which has continued to this day. The King James Bible was a part of most homes in America from colonial times, and it was read aloud by the fireside in the long dark evenings of the year. Although the Bible was also the source of entertaining stories and examples of moral behavior, it also became familiar background for the efforts of evangelical conversion.

Despite the incursions of more extreme evangelism, by the early nineteenth century in major population centers, religious orthodoxy was less tied to biblical interpretation than to respect for priestly authority and devotion to the tenets of Romanism and Calvinism. It was generally accepted that human beings were born in sin and were redeemed by Christ's suffering and sacrifice. Those educated in the traditions could disagree about determinism and salvation by works or by faith, but the central doctrine was firmly set: Human beings were flawed by virtue of Adamic disobedience and subsequent banishment from paradise. As a result, suffering in this world was the norm and the only hope was to pray for eventual salvation in Heaven, while fearing eternity in Hell. This dualistic doctrine runs deep in the psyche of all Christians regardless of denomination.

In his essay "Compensation" Emerson confronts dualism head on, making it the platform from which he takes his own stand on the truth of human nature. He begins the essay with the observation that he had always wanted to write on the thorny topic of Compensation—the laws of the universe as they apply to human nature and life—because it seemed to him that in this arena experience trumped Church doctrine. Here is his presentation of the orthodox position:

> I was lately confirmed in these desires [*to write on the subject*] by hearing a sermon at church. The preacher, a man esteemed for his orthodoxy, unfolded in the ordinary manner the doctrine of the Last Judgment. He assumed, that judgment is not executed in this world; that the wicked are successful; that the good are miserable; and then urged from reason and from Scripture a compensation to be made to both parties in the next life. No offence appeared to be taken by the congregation at this doctrine. As far as I could observe, when the meeting broke up, they separated without remark on the sermon.
>
> Yet what was the import of this teaching? What did the preacher mean by saying that the good are miserable in the present life? Was it that houses and lands, offices, wine, horses, dress, luxury, are had by unprincipled men, whilst the saints are poor and despised; and that a compensation is to be made to these last hereafter, by giving them the like gratifications another day, —bank-stock and doubloons, venison and champagne? This must be the compensation intended; for what else? Is it that they are to have leave to pray and praise? to love and serve men? Why, that they can do now. The legitimate inference the disciple would draw was, — 'We are to have such a good time as the sinners have now'; —or, to push it to its extreme import, —'You sin now; we shall sin by and by; we would sin now, if we could; not being successful, we expect our revenge to-morrow.'

These are central questions. What, finally, is God's involvement in human life? What is God's justice and how is it meted out? The orthodox answer to these questions rests on the doctrine of the Last Judgment, that God's time is different from our own and that *eventually*—and that is a very big word in these matters—eventually justice is done and evil punished.

Emerson's position, taken from his conviction that religion is based on the presence of a higher consciousness and not on biblical authority, is that justice in this world is immediate and entire. A crime or a sin is punished immediately within the individual. We are diminished as human beings immediately upon the commission of a crime. Our punishment is that we are separated from that source of divinity within us until such time as we acknowledge that separation and become, once more, a part of, or aligned with, the Source.

In Emerson's view it is not possible for an individual to enjoy the fruits of ill-gotten gains because of the constant presence of awareness of the crime. Only when we are free of such awareness, or guilt, can we experience freedom, contentment, and happiness. That others may see the individual free and living "the good life" is irrelevant. The inner world is what matters.

Here then, in this examination of one aspect of doctrinal debate, is the crux of the crisis of faith which resulted during the 1830s and 40s in the birth of Transcendentalism—which, in short, was an attempt to reconcile the differences and schisms of the fragmented world that Emerson experienced as a result of new scientific knowledge, new biblical research, and outmoded religious doctrines. His was an exercise in unification, bringing together in one new mode of thought all the insights achieved by human beings in philosophy, science, theology, and artistic expression.

It would take nearly thirty years before a strong conservative reaction set in to counter the perceived liberalism and so-called heresy of Transcendentalism, which in turn would transform itself into a literary rather than religious and spiritual movement. But even then it would not be until the early twentieth century before Fundamentalism would become a coherent movement and then another fifty years before it became a political force in American life.

When Emerson returned from Europe in October, 1833, after having formally resigned as a minister, he faced an uncertain future. He wrote in his journal, "I like my book on nature, and wish I knew where and how I ought to live." Within five years, he had published his manifesto *Nature;* delivered his Phi Beta Kappa Address at Harvard, "The American Scholar"; and had addressed the graduates of Divinity College with a sermon so powerful and theologically radical that he had effectively liberated himself from all orthodox religious forms. Finally, it was the essay "Self-Reliance" that captured the imagination of readers and established Emerson as a spokesman for a new mode of thinking and being. The rest of his work, as they say, is footnotes to these primary documents.

Emerson's published inquiries into the spiritual unknown would establish him as the father of American religious independence. His rhetoric in the name of spiritual freedom would support like-minded seekers in their quest to worship without mediation, finding truth within their own spiritual resources, and would spawn a hundred different movements and religious associations, informal and formal, throughout the country. But because of the principles laid down in "Self-Reliance" there would never be an Emersonian church.

At the same time, however, a reaction to the general crisis of faith was taking place in more conservative circles throughout the country, as ministers and Bible-loving citizens moved to re-establish the sanctity of God's Word as revelation and to re-affirm the literal word of scripture. Not until the appearance of a series of religious pamphlets in 1910–15, however, would the word *Fundamentalism* finally be coined to describe this movement. From then on, though—partly in response to liberalism in Church doctrine and partly to Emersonian individualism and to teaching Darwinian evolution in the nation's schools—a struggle for the soul of America emerged with distinct boundaries.

Today, this struggle has once again emerged for a nation in crisis, with religious belief a major combatant in a struggle for the soul of the nation. This struggle is more than conflict over cultural values, about the content of entertainment, about lifestyles, and about instruction in our schools. It is ultimately about the nature of truth itself and about the means of perceiving that truth. And despite those who believe that all truth is relative and no different from opinion, the issue of the nature of the truth of reality remains philosophically, spiritually, and scientifically relevant to many serious thinkers. Skeptics aside, the struggle to define and express the truth about the existence of God, the nature of matter and the universe, and the meaning of human life remains a vital interest, and those on the extremes of that struggle are having more and more influence in how the matter is ultimately going to be settled.

It may be useful in considering this crisis of faith to think about Europe as a contrast to American religious circumstances. The secularization of European culture has left that continent without a spiritual core. A recent book, *Reflections on the Revolution in Europe* by Christopher Caldwell, makes the point that the introduction of Moslem immigrants into Europe has created a crisis because a once-powerful Christian faith no longer exists. Caldwell quotes the German philosopher Jürgen Habermas, an atheist, who wrote: "Christianity, and nothing else, is the ultimate foundation of liberty, conscience, human rights, and democracy, the benchmarks of Western civilization. To this we have no other options. We continue to nourish ourselves from this source. Everything else is postmodern chatter."

I cannot in good conscience leave this subject without reference to a journal entry Emerson penned in 1834, very early in his career. It is a powerful sentiment and one never used in the *Complete Works*. In it, Emerson pleads for our dedication to the truth, in fact, to Idealism.

. . . whenever we live rightly, thought will express itself in ordinary action so fully as to make a special action, that is, a religious form, impertinent. Is not Solomon's temple built because Solomon is not a temple, but a brothel and a change-house? Is not the meeting-house dedicated because men are not? Is not the church opened and filled on Sunday because the commandments are not kept by the worshipers on Monday? But when he who worships there, speaks the truth, follows the truth, is the truth's; when he awakes by actual communion to the faith that God is in him, will he need any temple, any prayer? The very fact of worship declares that God is not at one with himself, that there are two gods. Now does this sound like high treason and go to lay flat all religion? It does threaten our forms; but does not that very word "form" already sound hollow? It threatens our forms, but it does not touch injuriously Religion. Would there be danger if there were real religion? . . . But the people, the people. You hold up your pasteboard religion for the people who are unfit for a true. So you say. But presently there will arise a race of preachers who will take such hold of the omnipotence of truth that they will blow the old falsehood to shreds with the breath of their mouth. There is no material show so splendid, no poem so musical as the great law of Compensation in our moral nature. When an ardent mind once gets a glimpse of that perfect beauty, and sees how it envelopes him and determines all his being, will he easily slide back to a periodic shouting about "blood atoning"? I apprehend that the religious history of society is to show a pretty rapid abandonment of forms of worship and the renovation and exaltation of preaching into real anxious instruction.

It is later, when he sat down to write "Self-Reliance," that Emerson dared to state the principle forcefully in the following sentence: "As men's prayers are a disease of the will, so are their creeds a disease of the intellect." His use of the word "disease" may seem harsh and extreme, but he is thinking about the price of spiritual health for both the will and the intellect. When we look closely at church attendance in America, the raw data seems to show that about 20 percent of Americans attend religious services on a regular basis. In contrast, more than 90 percent profess a faith in the existence of God. This contrast may be a reflection of Bloom's assertion that Emerson is indeed the father of the American

Religion, that Americans have their own personal faith, or as the ancient Greeks would say, their own household gods and their own way of communing with them, him, her, or it.

One aspect of the Dream of America is marked by this discrepancy between faith and practice. Our founders were more philosophic than religious. Freedom to worship meant more than freedom to choose which church to attend. It also meant freedom not to attend any and to decide for ourselves what role, if any, religion would play in our lives. Emerson's self-reliance was founded on just that freedom.

# 4
# The New Self-Reliance

"S ELF-RELIANCE" was Emerson's declaration of independence. It represented not just freedom from traditional religious forms, and the literary and cultural influence from England, which he had called for in "American Scholar," but was a declaration of individual independence from conformity of all kinds. It was in fact a call for the virtues and transformational power of self-trust. The essay has long been a staple of American culture, education, and personal inspiration. It is also a complex and deeply disturbing analysis of what it means to be an individual.

Most of our virtues, Emerson tells us, come from either religious penance or misplaced obligation, the outer pressure to conform to society's expectations. We are given awards, recognition, and dinners for our good works, but our inner lives remain untouched if these kudos are the aim of our actions. Emerson is tough here, and uncompromising. The language he employs seeks to unravel our self-satisfactions, and we are offended by hearing him say, "I grudge the dollar, the dime, the cent, I give to such men as do not belong to me and to whom I do not belong." Apologists defend Emerson by explaining and explaining again that he was a generous, giving man. Nonetheless, his demands on true character push against an easy set of societal virtues in order to strike a new note. "Character teaches above our wills. Men imagine that they communicate their virtue or vice only by overt actions, and do not see that virtue or vice emit a breath every moment."

As individuals and the nation currently face the crises that threaten our well-being, I first offer one paragraph from "Self-Reliance" as an assessment of the conformity that in spite of ourselves we cherish. Then I will offer another as a prescription for a new self-reliance, one which President Obama, who lists "Self-Reliance" as a pivotal essay in his own development, has also articulated. We begin in the middle of a paragraph describing the present conditions in which we live:

> Well, most men have bound their eyes with one or another handker-chief, and attached themselves to some one of these communities of opinion. This conformity makes them not false in a few particulars, authors of a few lies, but false in all particulars. Their every truth is not quite true. Their two is not the real two, their four not the real four; so that every word they say chagrins us, and we know not where to begin to set them right. Meantime nature is not slow to equip us in the prison-uniform of the party to which we adhere. We come to wear one cut of face and figure, and acquire by degrees the gentlest asinine expression. There is a mortifying experience in particular, which does not fail to wreak itself also in the general history; I mean "the foolish face of praise," the forced smile which we put on in company where we do not feel at ease in answer to conversation which does not inter-est us. The muscles, not spontaneously moved, but moved by a low usurping wilfulness, grow tight about the outline of the face with the most disagreeable sensation.

A "low usurping wilfulness" indeed. What can and must we do to break out of this prison? The first thing is to recognize that we have acquiesced in this imprisonment. It has been a choice we made early on and have fallen victim to its deadening habits, and it has been low, usurp-ing, and wilful. Often enough we awake to find ourselves waist deep in the quicksand of conformity and then it is too late. Pulling ourselves up by our own boot straps from quicksand won't work. We must be alert to that initial step into earth that is not firm beneath our feet.

Further along, Emerson's use of the word "party" describes not merely a political party or a communal group of like-minded associates, but all forms of collective identification, a clinging to some prescribed and clearly defined set of statements and attitudes within which we settle down and define ourselves. When leaders speak to us about being one people and one nation, they cannot mean as well one mind in the sense of collective group-think. When Emerson says, in the opening sentence of "History," "There is one mind common to all individual men," it is a universal mind to which he refers. It means access to what is true for everyone, the universal truth in which and through which we take our life.

The sense of "party" then, is set as a diminution of that universal mind to which we have access in quiet, solitary moments. Party assumes its other meanings as well, then. In our conformity, we are in and at a party, what Emerson means by "the forced smile we put on in company where we do not feel at ease in answer to conversation which does not interest us." More than mere social discomfort, Emerson's image describes all of our wilful conformity, at work and at play. That reaction is the central reason we choose our friends so carefully, so that we can feel genuine in company and can feel a certain authentic selfhood around others.

What then is to be done? How do we extricate ourselves from this false set of so-called virtues? Even Emerson, at this early stage of his creative life and even with his rich gifts of eloquence, is ambiguous, at times even opaque. It will take a full examination of his whole body of work to find the reality we seek, but here, in "Self-Reliance" is one measure of salutary assistance.

> Why, then, do we prate of self-reliance? Inasmuch as the soul is present, there will be power not confident but agent. To talk of reliance is a poor external way of speaking. Speak rather of that which relies,

because it works and is. Who has more obedience than I masters me, though he should not raise his finger. Round him I must revolve by the gravitation of spirits. We fancy it rhetoric, when we speak of eminent virtue. We do not yet see that virtue is Height, and that a man or a company of men, plastic and permeable to principles, by the law of nature must overpower and ride all cities, nations, kings, rich men, poets, who are not.

True self-reliance comes, then, from a power that is agent, that is, a power enabled through our very nature to act on behalf of our self-recovery from wilful conformity and the seductions of "party." To be enabled in this way takes obedience to the call of the soul, which in Emerson's vocabulary means that agent both within and without that speaks to us from the hidden universal source of life itself. Emerson might have said, in addition to the comment that "reliance is a poor external way of speaking," that the word "obedience" is also such a word. We use it most often in relation to obeying orders and demands from an external authority. We seldom think of it as obedience to an inner demand or self-generated authority. How can I be obedient to myself if I do not recognize my self as an authority to be obeyed? Clearly I cannot and will not.

Therefore, when Emerson insists that "who has more obedience than I masters me," he tells us where we stand in the process of developing and maintaining a true self-reliance. Persons who possess self-reliance command us because we recognize their authority and power over our weaker grasp of selfhood. In their presence we flounder, apologize, acquiesce, and follow, and they need not lift a finger. We find ourselves in an orbit not of our own making or choosing.

Emerson uses the capitalized word "Height" in this passage to characterize this power, suggestive of deity, not in the ordinary sense of a god above or a princely position on the hill, but rather from an elevated point of perception and an obedience to higher consciousness. "We do not yet see," he says, reminding us that this Height, as he calls it, is rarely attained and even more rarely sustained. We live in an elevated state of wisdom only in rare moments, but as he says in the opening sentences of "The Over-Soul,"

> There is a difference between one and another hour of life, in their authority and subsequent effect. Our faith comes in moments; our vice is habitual. Yet there is a depth in those brief moments which constrains us to ascribe more reality to them than to all other experiences.

And he ends that first paragraph by saying, "I am constrained every moment to acknowledge a higher origin for events than the will I call mine." And yet true self-reliance comes from an exercise of will and intellect on behalf of our self-recovery. Therefore his use of the sentence about prayer as a disease of the will helps to make the point about failure of will. If we see prayers as begging God for relief or salvation from a crisis, our self-will flounders in self-pity. Our strength comes when we see self-reliance and God-reliance as one.

I entitled this chapter "The New Self-Reliance" because it is clear now that since Emerson's first assertions of this theme nearly a hundred and seventy years ago, we may have assimilated personally and culturally some of the language and substance of his intention, but we have yet to manifest his words in matters of national character. To some extent some of the spiritual and self-development movements have absorbed this material and have formulated and reformulated its essence and principles into systems of enlightenment and self-recovery. What remains is the actual work and its realization to a larger sphere.

Unfortunately, this narrower development has also evolved into the presence of self-serving gurus merchandising what can never be sold or merchandised. Emerson himself has been reduced to a purveyor of slogans and aphorisms empty of meaning outside their context. And yet there remains a powerful essence coming from the man's words that has been absorbed and may now be put to work in the culture.

The election of 2008 and the presence of Barack Obama as a potential but as yet unproven leader attests to this fact. An example may make the point. One of the saddest and most telling moments in the campaign for the presidency took place when candidate Hillary Clinton tried without success to blunt Obama's eloquence as mere window dressing. In a sarcastic, ill-conceived speech, she said that because of Obama the heavens would open, angels would descend, choirs would sing, and everything would be all right and peace would break out all over the world. It was, in fact, a moment of profound frustration for her campaign. Eventually, she had the grace to acknowledge that what Obama was saying did not come from empty sentimentality or campaign rhetoric, but rather from an Emersonian Height, a place recognized by millions of Americans as authentic and relevant to their lives and to America's future.

The development of a language of self-recovery and the work done by millions of seekers and those devoted to self-development has resulted for many in a new, higher level of discrimination, the ability to separate life-enhancing wheat from empty chaff. This faculty of discrimination is what many perceived in Obama's eloquence and it is what Clinton was not able to mock successfully. And this same faculty is what makes Emersonian self-reliance something new and approachable.

In 1842, Emerson wrote "Experience," one of his most powerful and personally revealing essays. In it he referred to what he called "this new yet unapproachable America." We will see over the next few years if indeed this nation, conceived in liberty and promising so much to those who have fought and died to preserve its founding, shall perish from the Earth, as Lincoln said, or shall be finally approached. We will know more clearly whether what we see in this young, eloquent president can fulfil that promise.

# 5

# Idealism and the Perennial Philosophy

WE HAVE seen since the appearance of Barack Obama on the American political scene a revival of traditional idealism connected to progressive ideas and goals. Such a revival has been a long time coming, having been swept aside by free market capitalism as championed by Ronald Reagan. Conservatives in politics and the media were successful in branding liberalism as unrealistic, wasteful, ill-conceived, and philosophically unsound. The rebirth of idealism associated with public policy goals, including universal health care, environmental activism, social justice, gay and women's rights, to name just a few issues, has once again taken hold.

The important fact of this trend has not been merely the rebirth of idealism on the left, but more importantly the fact that idealism is being revived as valid social policy in opposition to firmly established conservative ideology. The reaction to the social upheavals of the Sixties and early Seventies has passed into history and a new kind of social and political activism has taken hold. As a direct result, Emerson's idealism has been revived as well.

What are the principles behind Emerson's philosophy and his vision of human self-development? What are the sources of the work he would have us do? Can we be confident that once undertaken, this work will yield the authenticity and truth we seek? These questions are important if we are to penetrate the unique vocabulary and rhetoric forged in his education, reading, and personal experience.

Emerson's idealism, what would later take on the title of New England Transcendentalism, came to him, he attests, "transcendentally" and was reinforced through his eclectic reading of both Eastern and Western sources. The primary confirmation, the test of his insights, was Platonic philosophy. In a later lecture, "Life and Literature," Emerson summarized this influence:

No doctrine has shown more vitality in this way than what is called the Platonic Philosophy. It had its own ancestry. Anaxagoras was the master of Socrates, Socrates of Plato, Plato of Aristotle; all the four, minds of original power, and of rare breadth and humanity, —pure power of thought clearing itself of the limits and traditions of the people, and trying its force on the problems of man and nature, with a courage and perception that yielded more memorable statements, more coherent particulars rounding into a theory of life and practice, than ever belonged to a movement which was essentially intellectual. Each of these minds stands for somewhat of his own; but Plato's best for what was intellectual and cosmical in the period. It consisted in the affirmation of the mind as the source of things: it taught an absolute unity. Being was first: Intellect, soul, matter, and the eternal generation of forms, worlds, and kinds. But Being or the first cause was moved to create, to the end of imparting happiness. All power, all good, all beauty, was in the mind. The soul, sufficient, could convert evil to good. Truth was the end and aim: he that had it was so far safe, immortal, and godlike.

Emerson wanted to be true to the idealist's vision that each age and period has its own revelation, so that when he came to write *Nature*, his purpose was to be true to that vision. The publication of *Nature* in 1836 did not make Emerson famous—far from it. The meager five hundred copies originally printed would take years to sell out, and only after the success of his lectures, addresses, and two more books of essays would *Nature* begin to find an audience more eager and, we must say, patient, to explore his work. *Nature* was obscure, too lofty for most, and generally only those who shared the transcendental vision in the first place found it satisfying. Even today, the central sections of the small book, chapters three through six to be exact, do not receive as much critical attention as the opening sections and the transcendent conclusion.

Chapter six, entitled "Idealism," presents what Emerson calls "the effects of culture," seen as evidence of the higher powers present behind the surfaces of nature. When Emerson uses the term "culture" in his work, he usually means self-culture, that process in life through which a human being exercises reflective attention through conscious awareness. Self-culture is the thought, action, and experience of spiritual (as opposed to religious) self-development. It is characteristic of our own time to think of culture as the patterns and effects of social structure, including the arts, beliefs, and institutions created by human thought and action. Emerson sought to expand this definition by including the dynamic processes within the individual of conscious being, thus to rehabilitate the idea of culture as ordinarily received.

In the process, Emerson places *Nature* within the orbit of what Leibnitz before him and Aldous Huxley later called the Perennial Philosophy, or what René Guénon and Ananda Coomaraswamy called simply "The Tradition." Connected to it, and also part of the common thread of its core vision is Advaita Vedanta, the Indian philosophy of non-duality, which for the past forty years or so has been recognized as integral to Emerson's thought.

The Perennial Philosophy has its roots in oral tradition going back into prehistory. It emerged in writing in the East before the Buddha and before Lao Tse and was later refined in India through Sankaracharya, the Indian philosopher who was in his prime around 800 c.e. In the West, the thread came fifteen hundred years earlier through the Pre-Socratic philosophers of Ionia, particularly Pythagoras and his school and Heraclitus and his fragments on the *Logos*. A dominant strain evolved in Plato and was developed fully by the Neo-Platonists: Plotinus, Proclus, and Iamblicus in particular. It came further into the West early in the Italian Renaissance through the patronage of Cosimo De Medici, his court philosopher Marcilio Ficino, and the young, brilliant Pico della Mirandola, whose Oration on the Dignity of Man gave the movement its overtones of individual human freedom. The thread then worked its way north into England around 1660 with the Cambridge Platonists John Smith and Ralph Cudworth, and hence to the Romantic authors and then to Channing and on to the Emerson circle in Concord.

A more direct connection to Emerson came through Thomas Taylor, the Platonist, whose translations of Plato's *Works* in English were published in 1803. Taylor subsequently translated many of the Neoplatonists as well. Emerson's editions of Taylor's Plato and Plotinus were well marked and equally well absorbed. Taylor was part of the company surrounding William Blake. He was self-taught in Greek, which caused him to be dismissed by the academic establishment in England; but he was supported in his work by several important patrons, including George and William Meredith, who recognized his genius. The significance of Taylor's work was that he made the esoteric connection between Plato and the Perennial Philosophy and in effect saved Plato for a devoted few from the ravages of academic reductionism, as evidenced by the translations of Jowett and Cairns.

In the essay "Intellect" Emerson left us a valuable record of his debt to the Perennial Philosophy in this passage:

> But I cannot recite, even thus rudely, laws of the intellect, without remembering that lofty and sequestered class of men who have been its prophets and oracles, the high-priesthood of the pure reason, the "Trismegisti", the expounders of the principles of thought from age to age. When, at long intervals, we turn over their abstruse pages,

wonderful seems the calm and grand air of these few, these great spiritual lords, who have walked in the world, —these of the old religion, —dwelling in a worship which makes the sanctities of Christianity look "parvenues" and popular; for "persuasion is in soul, but necessity is in intellect." This band of grandees, Hermes, Heraclitus, Empedocles, Plato, Plotinus, Olympiodorus, Proclus, Synesius, and the rest, have somewhat [read something] so vast in their logic, so primary in their thinking, that it seems antecedent to all the ordinary distinctions of rhetoric and literature, and to be at once poetry, and music, and dancing, and astronomy, and mathematics. I am present at the sowing of the seed of the world.

The power of the Perennial Philosophy is that it possesses common threads through uncommon times and cultural traditions. As opposed to all the major religions, which at their core assert the uniqueness of their founding and the absolute truth of their beliefs, the Perennial Philosophy is decidedly not, as its name suggests, a religion. Although various writers, including Huston Smith and Frithjof Schuon, have claimed that The Tradition, as it was named by Guénon and Coomaraswamy, forms the basis of religious belief, history only indirectly supports this claim.

The core of the Perennial Philosophy is the immanent presence of a divine reality at the ground of being. The Greek concept of the *logos,* combined with the notion of *nous,* or universal mind, gives the Perennial Philosophy its spiritual center in the western tradition, but the absence of dogma, founding sacred texts, devotional practice, particular prophets, or a spiritual founder such as Abraham, Jesus, or Mohammad, keeps it a philosophy. This detail is important to any further connection to Emerson because, as later chapters will argue, his intention was to separate himself from religious doctrine and to focus instead on the philosophy of Idealism as it directly pertained both to individuals and to America. In fact, more than any other vision of reality—for that is what it is—the Perennial Philosophy has at its core the foundation of Emerson's thought.

Another major difference between the Perennial Philosophy and doctrinal systems is its conviction that although the purpose of human life is to return spiritually to the essence of the divine Reality, this essence does not proclaim a personal god who participates in some way similar to human action in the affairs of nature and society. Rather, this essence is manifest in existence through laws and principles which cannot be altered or superseded. This divine reality may be experienced first through the laws of the universe, which include the laws of the mind, and its substance may be developed through practices such as meditation or quiet reflection, which, Idealism asserts, gives access to that reality or ground of being.

The present crisis in America has as its cause the failure to connect our founding with a universal reality based on these principles, despite the efforts of men like Washington, Jefferson, Adams, and Franklin to articulate those principles. Referring to Emerson as one of our founding thinkers is an attempt to make that connection, one which has been only marginally carried forward by leaders such as Franklin Roosevelt, John Kennedy, and now Barack Obama. Political leaders cannot sound too philosophical in this anti-intellectual environment, a fact leaving us with few options for "solving the times," as Emerson phrased it.

The question, then, is how can a spiritual philosophy be applied to find our way to a new and exceptional age? In his book *The Perennial Philosophy*, Aldous Huxley made the claim that as a metaphysical idea, the Perennial Philosophy "has a place" within the great religions, but he qualified his definition. Here is Aldous Huxley's description:

[The Perennial Philosophy is] the metaphysic that recognizes a divine Reality substantial to the world of things and lives and minds; the psychology that finds in the soul something similar to, or even identical with, divine Reality; the ethic that places man's final end in the knowledge of the immanent and transcendent Ground of all being; the thing is immemorial and universal. Rudiments of the perennial philosophy may be found among the traditional lore of primitive

peoples in every region of the world, and in its fully developed forms
it has a place in every one of the higher religions.

The qualification of "in its fully developed forms" suggests a forced
occupation, however, and we do not find in practice any such full development today, except in the private closets of spiritual seekers within
and without many faiths. This dislocation is important because in our
own time the inclination to find a comfort zone for the Perennial Philosophy within religious forms tends to negate The Tradition's aversion
to doctrine and lends credibility to the assumption that Emerson was
comfortable with such forms. He was not, as we shall see later.

In *Nature*'s "Idealism" chapter, Emerson established his own place
in the Perennial Philosophy in terms that progress from a bottom-up
sequence of insights. He begins with a separation of the illusory nature
of the world from the human perception of that illusion: "I may say,
a low degree of the sublime is felt from the fact, probably, that man
is hereby apprized, that, whilst the world is a spectacle, something in
himself is stable." Once we recognize the presence of our inner stability
in contrast to a world in constant flux, we find ourselves on a firmer
path to higher levels of perception. Plato spelled out the problem we
encounter as we begin our search. The problem of philosophy, according
to Plato, is, for all that exists conditionally, we seek to find a ground
unconditioned and absolute. It proceeds on the perception that law
determines all phenomena, which being known, the phenomena can be
predicted. We search for the fixed laws.

Emerson puts his finger directly on the problem. Without a place
to stand, with its unconditional and absolute ground of being, we are
forced to build on the shifting sands of relativism, and then, whatever
we hold to be true in one place and time is not true somewhere else
in another time. Morality then becomes local and dependent on local
laws and customs. Or, worst, it becomes the province of ideologues, who
seize upon the vacated ground to build monuments to themselves and
then prisons for those who express an aversion to their version of the

truth. The world today is choked with such monuments and prisons.

In the same paragraph Emerson continues the argument and from poetic inspiration shifts to physics—surprising for a former minister, but also prophetic in light of of developments in the twentieth century.

> Is not the charm of one of Plato's or Aristotle's definitions, strictly like that of the *Antigone* of Sophocles? It is, in both cases, that a spiritual life has been imparted to nature; that the solid seeming block of matter has been pervaded and dissolved by a thought; that this feeble human being has penetrated the vast masses of nature with an informing soul, and recognised itself in their harmony, that is, seized their law. In physics, when this is attained, the memory disburthens itself of its cumbrous catalogues of particulars, and carries centuries of observation in a single formula.

This line of reasoning prefigures Maxwell and Einstein's equivalence of matter and energy, and then startlingly, the following one anticipates quantum theory. The observation that "Intellectual science has been observed to beget invariably a doubt of the existence of matter" leads directly to the insight that matter is constituted of fields of energy and from there into the paradox of the infinite power residing in the vacuum of space. Emerson would have been quietly satisfied that his philosophical position was to be empirically confirmed. Matter, indeed, does not exist in the absolute sense in which we normally define reality. And yet there must be, and is, a reality founded on the laws that create and sustain the universe or multi-verses, as the case may well be.

In his time, Emerson was forced by developments in science to find examples of a reality behind and beyond matter in less than moving terms:

> Thus even in physics, the material is degraded before the spiritual. The astronomer, the geometer, rely on their irrefragable analysis, and disdain the results of observation. The sublime remark of Euler on his law of arches, "This will be found contrary to all experience, yet

is true;" had already transferred nature into the mind, and left matter like an outcast corpse.

Although Euler's law of arches served a purpose here, it was only barely the stuff of transcendence, no matter the awe with which we greet the genius of Roman bridge builders and the fact that Euler's laws continue to generate scientific papers. For us, however, the quantum world and Einstein's equivalence of matter and energy illustrate more dramatically the ambiguity of material reality.

The connection of this ambiguity to the Perennial Philosophy is less easily made. Again, Emerson uses the unusual figure of the French economist and philosopher Jacques Turgot to support his thesis: "Turgot said, 'He that has never doubted the existence of matter, may be assured he has no aptitude for metaphysical inquiries.'" The use of the term "metaphysics" here is still seen by many as a quaint glimpse into the past, now that modern philosophy has followed Wittgenstein's dictum that we have no empirical basis to discuss metaphysics. There is, however, enough ambiguity in the later Wittgenstein to suggest that he might have been in the forefront of a new metaphysics had he lived longer.

When Emerson says beginning the same paragraph, "Intellectual science has been observed to beget invariably a doubt of the existence of matter," he uses the word "intellectual" in contradistinction to the reductionism of the scientific method. Another example of that same usage is found in Coomaraswamy, when he says, "The weakness of the scientific position is, not that empirical facts are devoid of interest or utility, but that these facts are thought of as a refutation of the *intellectual* doctrine. [italics mine]"

Because Emerson was writing primarily in the 1830s and 1840s, metaphysical speculation had yet to fall completely to the onslaught of The Age of Realism (1865–1910) and to the reductionism in philosophy coming from the Vienna Circle after 1920. As a result of a lingering respect for metaphysics, Emerson did not have to write defensively, even though he found himself founder of a tiny movement to be known as

New England Transcendentalism, which is in its particulars and its core a metaphysical doctrine.

In our own time, the Perennial Philosophy holds greater sway than the more narrow New England Transcendentalism of *Nature* because its traditions are longer and deeper. It is also true that Emerson's more overt metaphysical language tends to be off-putting to those seeking a more contemporary spiritual philosophy. And yet when we read with a penetrating eye, sifting through Emerson's ministerial language in most sections, the attentive reader is able to find in the eloquence a means of fusing the Transcendental with the Perennial.

Emerson sums up chapter six of *Nature* with a plea for Idealism. It is a measured plea and takes its tone from the relative peace and natural tranquility of his own Concord life. Today, his tone would be different, more aggressive as well as more deeply pleading. See how this language understates the urgency of our current climate.

> The advantage of the ideal theory over the popular faith, is that it presents the world in precisely that view which is most desirable to the mind. It is, in fact, the view which Reason, both speculative and practical, that is, philosophy and virtue, take. For, seen in the light of thought, the world always is phenomenal; and virtue subordinates it to the mind.

In saying "most desirable to the mind" Emerson first means his own mind as he struggled through those early years of anguish and doubt from within the "popular faith" of his day. But he also means the greater mind, the realm of consciousness that Idealism sees as universal and which empirical science is even now inching towards with its own anguish, doubt, and curiosity. But Reason, the term used by Coleridge and the German Idealists, is the arbiter of truth in the matter, and since their sense of Reason is the highest faculty of the human mind, it is the faculty which seizes upon the intellectual doctrines as knowledge and transmits its perceptions to the understanding.

Finally, Emerson asserts that it is *virtue* that subordinates the phenomenal world to the mind, and here, once again, the modern reader runs into a changed view of virtue. It is in the "Divinity School Address" that Emerson defines virtue not as behavior but as "a reverence and delight in the presence of certain divine laws." It is, in other words, a perception or a stance in consciousness synonymous with both spiritual awareness and an evolved conscience, which in turn comes not from teaching (or tuition) but from insight (or intuition).

This meaning of virtue tells us once again that Emerson has translated the ordinary usages of traditional religious terminology into the language of self-culture. Therefore, virtue is not "good behavior" as much as it is a living relationship to "certain divine laws." Behavior is a matter of character, not of conformity to standards, and virtue becomes a possession of those who experience the feeling of reverence and delight in divine presence. It is in this way, then, that Emerson's testimony of being "part or parcel of God" in *Nature* becomes his place to stand and the platform from which he undertakes self-recovery.

The connection between Emerson's use of the word "virtue" and the Perennial Philosophy is also found in the work of Marcilio Ficino. In that fifteenth-century context, the Latin word *virtu* meant "the individual's total development of himself beyond all limits and the shaping of his life into a work of art."

In chapter 10 we will have more to say about Emerson's radical departure from the religious traditions of his day and the more evangelical movements of the American West and South. Our next chapter takes Idealism into the realm of Applied Principle, in three pivotal essays: "Spiritual Laws," "The Over-Soul," and "Circles."

# 6

# The Perennial Philosophy
# Applied

I F WE could have any security against moods! If the profoundest
prophet could be holden to his words, and the hearer who is ready
to sell all and join the crusade, could have any certificate that tomorrow
his prophet shall not unsay his testimony! But the Truth sits veiled
there on the Bench, and never interposes an adamantine syllable; and
the most sincere and revolutionary doctrine, put as if the ark of God
were carried forward some furlongs, and planted there for the succor
of the world, shall in a few weeks be coldly set aside by the same
speaker, as morbid; "I thought I was right, but I was not."

RWE, "Nominalist and Realist," *Essays II*

Should we listen to a teacher who says, "I thought I was right, but I was
not"? Can he be relied upon to say what is true for himself and for us
all? If we are to listen to Emerson, a man who humbly counts himself
in this company, what are we hearing? The brief essay "Nominalist and
Realist" in *Essays II,* was an effort to warn his readers to listen fully,
with care, to attend to his words with discrimination, and to look to the

firm insights and not the apologetic instance. So, too, with life itself. We must learn discrimination. The goal after all is to be able to listen to ourselves.

The essays of the First Series were powerful evocations of his vision, recorded in moments of inspiration at a very high level of perception. They were greeted variously by critical reviewers whose understanding differed strongly from Emerson's. He was not stung with these criticisms, far from it. He knew exactly what storms of protest he would create, just as he knew that his remarks on the state of Christianity at Divinity College years before would be greeted by cries of heresy.

Readers have to judge for themselves whether or not what I call the Ground of Being essays— "Spiritual Laws," "The Over-Soul," and "Circles" —resonate with their mood, as Emerson puts it, as evocations of a higher truth. These three Ground of Being essays describe the idealism of unity in the face of the polarities of ordinary life and, in addition, challenge the prevailing materialist theories of reality. This latter version of reality, our common experience, is Emerson's primary target in "Self-Reliance," "Experience," and "Compensation."

After the "transparent eye-ball" revelation in *Nature*, Emerson was more circumspect in publishing his mystical experiences. Yet such experiences form an important part of his perceptual framework. He also understood, as we see in "Nominalist and Realist" that no one person has a firm grasp of the true nature of truth and that all we experience are hints and glances of a greater, more coherent reality. But having been warned, we can approach the revelatory essays like "Spiritual Laws" with greater awareness and confidence.

These essays offer guidance to individuals lost in a crisis of faith, battered from all sides by uncertainties and proselytizing pronouncements. Prior to their publication in 1841, five years after *Nature*, material from "Over-Soul" and "Spiritual Laws" had been tested in the lecture hall, not as we see them, but as part of a series entitled "The Philosophy of History." By 1840, when he was assembling *Essays: First Series*, "Spiritual Laws" and "The Over-Soul" would form the overtly spiritual pieces in the series and be joined by way of a coda with "Circles," which contains the most original and untested material of the series.

## Spiritual Laws

"Spiritual Laws" begins with a grammatical sleight of hand. "When the act of reflection takes place in the mind . . ." passively states the process through which spiritual insight penetrates human consciousness. The infusion takes place unbidden. We do not instigate it through an act of will. The mind has its laws, and grammar is the set of fundamental laws that both shapes and reflects these processes. Syntax reflects how the mind works in accordance with higher laws. Sometimes we think actively, and sometimes a thought arises unbidden. When we think, we employ the calculating and planning mind. When a thought occurs unbidden, the intuitive faculty is at work. The mind also plays, dabbles, and runs amok, at which point "we" have to take control and bid it still itself. What is the difference then between reflected thought and aimless "stuff" that so often fills the restless mind?

The act of reflection takes place in the mind and "we look at ourselves in the light of thought." Again, reflection takes place and we are then allowed to observe ourselves in the light provided by what arises. The grammar here turns active. We (consciously) look at ourselves out of the darkness in the light of thought and in this clarity we are held in beauty because the soul "will not know either deformity or pain."

This process—and it is always process that concerns Emerson—is the means by which we achieve a stilling perspective in the midst of chaos. Not having the wherewithal to bring the mind to stillness so that the act of reflection can take place is the curse of modern life. Bringing the mind to such stillness is the practical goal of those who practice meditation. When Emerson chose to leave Boston and settle in the peace and quiet of Concord, he was ensuring the conditions necessary for a reflective life. It is hard for us to imagine that Boston in 1835 was so crowded and so distracting as to drive him to an inland sanctuary, but the wide reach of unspoiled nature was crucial to his journey.

As we move deeper into "Spiritual Laws" the question arises, What is it that comes to mind that we can trust and follow when the act of reflection takes place? Emerson's answer comes in a remarkable outburst of transcendental Idealism. I have included the entire passage, beginning "A little consideration of what takes place. . .), four paragraphs long, in Appendix I (see page 151) for readers not familiar with the contents. What is remarkable about the passage is its timeless lyricism, as if it were being sung or chanted, although we are uncertain if it was ever read in its present form from the lectern. It is one of Emerson's most overt efforts to advise, to set out principles by which an individual may sift through the so-called choices of life's journey.

On many occasions, I have used these paragraphs in classes and workshops to begin a discussion of how we might use the powers of intuition and what Emerson called "lowly listening" to sift through the mess of conflicting messages and influences that normally directs our decisions in life. Emerson's clear and clean prescription, tested and retested in experience, eases these conflicts considerably. Certainly one of its salient features is clarity.

One difficulty arises immediately when Emerson says, "by contenting ourselves with obedience we become divine." One can easily see how the Religious Right would seize upon this phrase as a vindication of biblical and ministerial authority, whereas Emerson means something entirely different by it. He refers to obeying the intimations of reflective thought, of the talents we are given, and the impulses which arise from thoughtful consideration. We become divine or akin to the divine through this obedience to the principles of self-trust, and not from any external human authority, much less through doctrinal authority.

It is tempting, nonetheless, to excuse Emerson for his use of this phrasing, and yet, he means obedience in the strict sense of the word. As he says in "Worship," "And so I think that the last lesson of life, the choral song which rises from all elements and all angels, is, a voluntary obedience, a necessitated freedom." Americans, like most freedom-loving people, have a natural resistance to being obedient. The word is associated with all kinds of enforced behaviors and uncomfortable social and familial relations. When Emerson uses an oxymoron like voluntary obedience or necessitated freedom, he shifts our mechanical thinking away from habitual action and reaction to set a new standard. As Cavell says, it is the "attractive and repellant way he writes."

By the time Emerson says, "The whole course of things goes to teach us faith . . . we need only obey," we are more likely to be on his wavelength. It is true that we tend to agonize over fundamental life-decisions involving profession, choice of mate, place to live, and even style of life. Many of these choices rush at us from external influences: parents, teachers, peers, and culture. Emerson wants us to step back, find solitude, listen to the inner voice, and follow the leadings of "lowly listening." And it is not God's will in any traditional sense that we are listening for, at least not in the way that phrase is employed in traditional religious contexts. It is the virtue of self-culture, that feeling of reverence we feel in the presence of divine laws. It is a spiritual feeling within the context of reflective thought.

The phrase "God wants me to . . ." creates nothing but trouble. Emerson heard this kind of religious fanaticism often in his day, and it is remarkable that errors of this kind did not fade away in time but actually have increased. The warning from Emerson to us is clear:

> Every man has this call of the power to do somewhat unique, and no man has any other call. The pretense that he has another call, a summons by name and personal election and outward "signs that mark him extraordinary, and not in the roll of common men," is fanaticism, and betrays obtuseness to perceive that there is one mind in all the individuals, and no respect of persons therein.

As he phrased it in his Divinity School Address, "the soul knows no persons." And it is certainly frightening to hear a former president of the United States say that God called him to be president. George W. Bush's exact statement was, "I feel like God wants me to run for

President. I can't explain it, but I sense my country is going to need me. Something is going to happen. . . . I know it won't be easy on me or my family, but *God wants me to do it.*" This kind of regal "divine right" creates an arrogance that leads to nothing but excess and, as we have witnessed, a stubborn disregard for the facts.

Therefore, what is the distinction to be drawn here? On one hand we are to listen humbly to an intuitive sense or presence within to discover our calling in life, a calling shown to us initially by our natural talents, which are based on our "organization," the way in which the general soul or universal mind incarnates itself in us. This language is opposed by the dualistic syntax of "God's will for us" and a direct leading by an active, personal spirit. It is easy to see, looking at the results of the latter, how fanaticism arises when an individual is convinced that the great God of the universe has sent a personal message to act in a certain way in a given situation. And yet, of course, millions of believers will affirm just this kind of belief, if only to affirm the existence of this presence in their lives.

"Each man has his own vocation. The talent is the call." It should be clear enough that talent not only informs but dictates many life decisions. Sadly, however, when talent is not exceptional, not at the level of genius, it is often not recognized, much less developed. Since our educational system is geared to uniformity and conformity, schools do not dedicate time and effort to identifying talent, except when it meets their own internal needs, such as in picking our potential athletes or class leaders. But now that we know that many different kinds of talents—physical, artistic, social, and intellectual—reside within most children, it is tragic that our educational system does not devote itself to uncovering them.

Emerson knew that once natural talent is recognized and developed, we "create the taste by which we are enjoyed." This last point is an important connection between the principles of self-reliance and the development of personal vocation. If schools were really able to fulfil their oft-stated goal of truly educating each individual to her or his potential, the place to start would be to tease out each child's talent through varied group activities and subject areas and then to begin to encourage and develop unique individual expression. Instead, we have focused our educational policies on uniformity (educating responsible citizens for the job market) while neglecting individual genius, which by Emerson's definition includes the talents to be cherished. Regardless of their stated goals, very few schools actually succeed in applying Emerson's principle with any consistency. Those interested can examine the Waldorf system for a glimpse into how this principle can be successfully applied.

At the close of this lyrical passage, Emerson says what indeed the passage does and what we should do: "let out all the length of all the reins . . . [and] find or make a frank and hearty expression of what force and meaning" is in us. The result of this release is to define what a human being can be in terms sadly unfamiliar to many of us. He says that a man is "a method, a progressive arrangement; a selecting principle, gathering his like to him, wherever he goes." The effect of these odd-sounding abstractions being applied to ourselves challenges us to consider in what way we are a method, a progressive arrangement, and a selecting principle. The challenge is in the nature of an elevation to a higher platform. These terms in effect take us out of ourselves while leaving us whole.

If I am a method, then it must be to accomplish something, as a sculptor uses the lost wax *method* to achieve the desired molding of an image. I am a method, or procedure to accomplish something according to a means. On the other hand, meditation is a method by which to still the mind and enter a different state of consciousness. But if I myself am a method, a progressive *arrangement,* then it must be to arrive eventually, through being what I am, to something different from what I conceive myself now to be. I am a progress as well as a person.

As to what a "selecting principle" might be, we find an answer in the phrase "gathering his like to him, wherever he goes." Being what we are and might become, we attract like energy and substance to us and can measure our advancements by the company we attract naturally to us and what we elect to keep. And all good company provides a context in which to maintain whatever progress we are able to make with our talents, our calling, and the taste by which we are enjoyed.

## The Over-Soul

For any ardent seeker, "The Over-Soul" is a prayer answered. It lays out with great clarity and compassion Emerson's personal vision of divinity and the meaning of the word "spiritual"—simply, a relation to that Unity, that Soul at the center of the universe. The essay begins with a declaration so vivid and clear that no careful reader can lose the train of thought or miss the essentials of the metaphysical mystery at the core.

"The Over-Soul" renews the principle of mystery at the center of spiritual knowledge. "Man is a stream whose source is hidden." Biological explanations notwithstanding, we begin as we end in mystery. Emerson's divine reality is immanent but unknowable, except in hints arising as insight as the result of an "alien energy" to the mind where the faculty of Reason begins its task of translation to the inferior Understanding. This last formulation arose for Emerson in a variety of contemporary sources, including Coleridge, Frederick Hedge, and Sampson Reed, whose "Observations on the Growth of the Mind" stimulated Emerson's thoughts on the topic of consciousness.

The central revelation of "The Over-Soul" is contained in its third paragraph:

> The Supreme Critic on the errors of the past and the present, and the only prophet of that which must be, is that great nature in which we rest, as the earth lies in the soft arms of the atmosphere; that Unity, that Over-soul, within which every man's particular being is contained and made one with all other; that common heart, of which all sincere conversation is the worship, to which all right action is submission; that overpowering reality which confutes our tricks and talents, and constrains every one to pass for what he is, and to speak from his char-

acter, and not from his tongue, and which evermore tends to pass into our thought and hand, and become wisdom, and virtue, and power, and beauty. We live in succession, in division, in parts, in particles. Meantime within man is the soul of the whole; the wise silence; the universal beauty, to which every part and particle is equally related; the eternal ONE. And this deep power in which we exist, and whose beatitude is all accessible to us, is not only self-sufficing and perfect in every hour, but the act of seeing and the thing seen, the seer and the spectacle, the subject and the object, are one. We see the world piece by piece, as the sun, the moon, the animal, the tree: but the whole, of which these are the shining parts, is the soul. Only by the vision of that Wisdom can the horoscope of the ages be read, and by falling back on our better thoughts, by yielding to the spirit of prophecy which is innate in every man, we can know what it saith.

Emerson was certainly aware of the extremes of religious enthusiasm and misinterpretation which would be spawned by the ecstatic outburst he allowed himself to record. As a result of this potential, his next task was to clarify the revelation to bring it into the realm of good sense and practice. He addresses this concern in a long passage about the nature of revelation and what he calls the "low curiosity" typical of the spiritualism rampant in his day. The vexing question of the immortality of the soul results in a wall of separation rising between the finite human soul and the infinite universal one. That separation produces anxiety, loneliness and fear. It is at the close of the following passage that Emerson repeats again the principle of unity or non-duality that is the hallmark of the Perennial Philosophy:

These questions which we lust to ask about the future are a confession of sin. God has no answer for them. No answer in words can reply to a question of things. It is not in an arbitrary "decree of God," but in the nature of man, that a veil shuts down on the facts of to-morrow; for the soul will not have us read any other cipher than that of cause and effect. By this veil, which curtains events, it instructs the children of men to live in to-day. The only mode of obtaining an answer to these questions of the senses is to forego all low curiosity, and, accepting the tide of being which floats us into the secret of nature, work and live, work and live, and all unawares the advancing soul has built and forged for itself a new condition, and the question and the answer are one.

Here is Emerson as seer. His answer to the perplexing questions of existence is to rise above the low curiosity of particulars and insist on dwelling in "the tide of being which floats us." This non-dualistic transcendentalism may not strike us as fully satisfying given the polarities of our lives, but non-duality is in fact the hallmark of the truth of reality. This fact begs the question, How then do we find ourselves confronted at every turn with these polarities? How are we to escape the tensions of what appear to be these endemic dualistic forces? If, as Emerson clearly admits, our experience consists not of long passages of unity but, rather, fragments, separation, tensions, and bits and pieces, how are we to find the unity? And the older we get (I can tell you) the more fragmented we feel as the body turns south and the mind seeks the northern reaches of detachment and serenity.

"The Over-Soul" confirms this separation and fragmentation while negating its ultimate reality. Our experience deceives us, Emerson says, and our senses lie. "Seeing is believing" is an impression of flawed vision. If reality is this great soul within which we take our life, then where are the moments of insight and clarity that reflect that unity? And isn't religious faith an affirmation and a practical solution to the impossibility of seeing truly?

Emerson's own "transparent eye-ball" experience in *Nature* has its apotheosis in the unitive declaration, "I see all; I am part or parcel of God." The moment came by surprise, walking in Boston Common on a November evening, with snow puddles dotting the green. There was no expectation, no anticipation of transcendent experience. It came unbidden. It was grace. If we seek supportive assurances of this oneness at the ground of being, we have two valuable paths we can take. On the one hand, we can explore the mystical tradition of the ancient texts of the Perennial Philosophy; or, more empirically, we can explore the cutting edge of the New Physics.

Before we take that deeper look into the new explorations of physics and consciousness, we need to let Emerson complete his thought in "The Over-Soul." The final paragraph is as direct an attack on traditional religious forms as he would allow himself to make. He says, "The reliance on authority measures the decline of religion, the withdrawal of the soul." In this case, authority builds a wall between the worshiper and the Over-Soul. The wall of authority creates a duality in which the authority figure or icon stands in for the subtle reality being sought, and the result is inevitably otherness and separation. In addition, when spiritual authority takes on the symbols of power, the separation is complete.

Faced with this wall, reminiscent of Plato's cave, we worship the dancing shadows, we carve images, we write dogmatic texts or tuck small prayers between the stones. We do everything except to take the radical step of turning away from the wall to seek the light of day and to open the field of spiritual experience to view.

Emerson anticipates the next step by declaring, "the universe is represented in an atom, in a moment of time. . . . a divine unity." This observation begins his revision of perception, his own radical insight into the nature of space and time. It also signals a change in emphasis from the soul of religious experience to the soul of natural science. His instinct to make that shift is also reflected in "Circles," the last of the three Ground of Being essays.

## Circles

"Circles" is both summary and transition. In the first paragraph we see the imposition of the instincts of a naturalist on the training of a cleric. "St. Augustine described the nature of God as a circle whose centre was everywhere, and its circumference nowhere." We may, perhaps, forgive Emerson for misquoting St. Augustine here. His journal for July, 1835 (JMN V, 56–57) suggests some misalignment of his notes, but the intention in "Circles" is clearly to attribute an example of natural law to a revered religious figure in order to begin shifting the ground of his argument. A year before (JMN IV, 381) he had written in his journal, "Every truth is a full circle." He had also said in a number of places that his efforts to describe the nature of the truth could describe only a small arc in its great circle. Human beings have their own small circles of growth and change, and at certain moments, if we are fortunate, we inscribe a larger circle in our self-recovery. "Our life is an apprenticeship to the truth, that around every circle another can be drawn."

The third paragraph sets the essential tone of the essay. The following passage possesses vision, grace, and sympathy in its fluid poetry:

> There are no fixtures in nature. The universe is fluid and volatile. Permanence is but a word of degrees. Our globe seen by God is a transparent law, not a mass of facts. The law dissolves the fact and holds it fluid. Our culture is the predominance of an idea which draws after it this train of cities and institutions. Let us rise into another idea: they will disappear. The Greek sculpture is all melted away, as if it had been statues of ice; here and there a solitary figure or fragment remaining, as we see flecks and scraps of snow left in cold dells and mountain clefts, in June and July. For the genius that created it creates now somewhat else. . . . The life of man is a self-evolving circle, which, from a ring imperceptibly small, rushes on all sides outwards to new and larger circles, and that without end. The extent to which this generation of circles, wheel without wheel, will go, depends on the force or truth of the individual soul. . . . Fear not the new generalization. Does the fact look crass and material, threatening to degrade thy theory of spirit? Resist it not; it goes to refine and raise thy theory of matter just as much.

The higher the platform we inhabit, the more fluid and less adamant we find the world, making it not only fluid but progressive. Emerson's plea here is a mind tolerant with change, a dissolution of barriers and the skepticism that prevents something new from entering our awareness. He then gives us a startling warning. "I am always insincere," he declares, "as always knowing there are other moods." What could be more fluid? If we, in turn, are fixed in our own little circle, what are we to make of such a remark? In the next paragraph he says, 'The new statement is always hated by the old, and, to those dwelling in the old, comes like an abyss of skepticism." In effect, he is playing with us, challenging us to be wary of fixed opinions or positions.

In fact, what appear to be contradictions in Emerson's work is the process of moving deeper not into the abyss of skepticism but rather the abyss of reality. Late in his career he wrote this in his journal for September 15, 1866: "I am here to be worked upon. There may be two or three or four steps, according to the genius of each, but for every seeing soul there are two absorbing facts, —I and the Abyss." The abyss is dark and deep to be sure and may be fearsome at first.

When Emerson asks us not to fear the new generalization, he is asking a great deal of us. He is asking us to keep growing, to not settle for the little enclosed circle where we are content, but rather to keep spiraling outward. And he accomplishes this by employing this shape-shifting language that challenges us as it makes us uneasy, even lightheaded. It is absolutely necessary, however, especially if we are prone to need the security of a fixed position. This theme of fluidity, change, and mood found expression in one of Emerson's extraordinary paragraphs in its perception of the human condition:

> Our moods do not believe in each other. Today I am full of thoughts, and can write what I please. I see no reason why I should not have the same thought, the same power of expression, to-morrow. What I write, whilst I write it, seems the most natural thing in the world; but yesterday I saw a dreary vacuity in this direction in which now I see so much; and a month hence, I doubt not, I shall wonder who he was that wrote so many continuous pages. Alas for this infirm faith, this

will not strenuous, this vast ebb of a vast flow! I am God in nature; I am a weed by the wall.

As a writer who demanded nothing less than eloquence and vision from his own pen, Emerson was conscious of the vicissitudes of the writer's craft, of its mysterious movements of vacuity and sudden outbursts of insight. And within that mystery it is the writing itself that characterizes the conscious nature of the examined life. His assertion, "I am God in nature" is overthrown by identification with the weed by the wall, short circuiting any accusation of overweening pride, although in Emerson's case the cries of heresy came nonetheless.

We are a mass of contradictions and countervailing impulses. An observation like "We thirst for approbation, yet cannot forgive the approver" cuts to the quick. Such is the nature of this spiritual work we do that "Every personal consideration that we allow costs us heavenly state." It is no wonder that we fret about making the effort at self-improvement. The price seems too great, given the personal stakes.

> Beware when the great God lets loose a thinker on this planet. Then all things are at risk. It is as when a conflagration has broken out in a great city, and no man knows what is safe, or where it will end. There is not a piece of science, but its flank may be turned to-morrow; there is not any literary reputation, not the so-called eternal names of fame, that may not be revised and condemned. The very hopes of man, the thoughts of his heart, the religion of nations, the manners and morals of mankind, are all at the mercy of a new generalization. Generalization is always a new influx of the divinity into the mind. Hence the thrill that attends it.

A new generalization comes from a great mind. The generalization becomes focused as a theory, which is rejected by the world, but when pieces of the theory are found to be facts, the theory is gradually accepted as reality. Here is such a generalization arising from Emerson's vision of reality: *The ground of being of the universe is not matter but is spirit, or rather, consciousness.* As we shall see in the next chapter, this aspect of Idealism ceased to be in the twentieth century a fundamental tenet of religion as practiced in America. Part of the reason for this was the overwhelming influence of Sigmund Freud and his transformation of consciousness into something suspect and hidden in the shadows of the unconscious. It was not until mid-century that the work of Carl Jung and the influence of Eastern religion and philosophy returned consciousness to its rightful place.

But it was in the beginning of the century, in the Einstein revolution in physics, that men such as Edwin Schrödinger and Wolfgang Pauli looked back into the ancient texts and saw the connections between what they were observing in quantum effects and the role of consciousness. Their insights brought new generalizations and shifted the focus away from materialism to give Idealism a new and more tangible foundation.

# 7

# Modern Physics and Theories of Consciousness

A MAN is the faculty of reporting, and the universe is the possibility of being reported.

RWE, *Representative Men*, "Goethe; or, the Writer"

The Perennial Philosophy was refined by Emerson and directed to questions of how human beings understand both themselves and the world. In the twentieth century, questions of human consciousness began to acquire a more empirically scientific basis, beginning, at least in Boston, with William James:

Out of my experience, such as it is (and it is limited enough) one fixed conclusion dogmatically emerges, and that it this, that we with our lives are like islands in the sea, or like trees in the forest. The maple and pine may whisper to each other with their leaves, and Conanicut [*sic*] and Newport hear each other's foghorns. But the trees also commingle their roots in the darkness underground, and the islands also hang together through the ocean's bottom. Just so there is a continuum of cosmic consciousness, against which our individuality builds but accidental fences, and into which our several minds plunge us into a mother-sea or reservoir. Our "normal" consciousness is circumscribed for adaptation to our external earthly environment, but the fen is weak in spots, and fitful influences from beyond leak in, showing the otherwise unverifiable common connection. Not only psychic research, but metaphysical philosophy, and speculative biology are led in their own ways to look with favor on some such "panpsychic" view of the universe as this.

A hundred years now after James' invocation of Emersonian cosmic consciousness, with our advancements in material science and in the presence of a universe too large and complex to comprehend—not to mention the possibility of other universes and dimensions hovering in our future discoveries—human existence in such vastness seems without meaning, at least in that largest of contexts. It was not a problem faced generally by people living a hundred years ago when James was doing his best work. The universe then seemed a more comfortable context in which our life could be lived with convincing coherence. Most people thought the universe consisted only of our own Milky Way galaxy, in which a finite number of stars moved in an orderly pattern through the millennia. There was no need to ponder supernovas or black holes or the implications of billions and billions of everything, including (quite literally) countless galaxies like our own.

The curious thing is that from the beginning the Perennial Philosophy and other esoteric teachings from various cultures nonetheless saw and understood the vastness of the universe and spoke without distress of infinitude as the fundamental basis of reality. Emerson himself grasped the notion of infinitude. Although not cognizant of the extent of space/time, he would not have been surprised by the discoveries of twentieth-century physics and astronomy. Genius tends to work that way.

For the most part, however, the great discoveries begun by Einstein and Hubble had little influence on the general population through mid-twentieth century. That all changed with the first explosions of the atomic bomb and the first pictures of Earth taken by astronauts from the Moon. Within a span of thirty years, modern physics became culturally relevant. Nowadays PBS runs specials on Superstring Theory and dark energy and matter, especially during pledge week, so popular have such programs become.

Ever since the publication of popularizing accounts such as *The Dancing Wu Li Masters* and *The Tao of Physics,* both published at the height of the New Age movement in the mid-Seventies, non-professionals have been paying much closer attention to developments in what we now call the New Physics. What this attention has meant, of course, is a virtual torrent of books over the last thirty years drawing conclusions ranging from the sensibly speculative to the irresponsibly outrageous about what quantum mechanics and the behavior of sub-atomic particles means for the study of ultimate reality, consciousness, and even the meaning of human existence.

To date, although much of the writing has been immensely interesting, no one has made a definitive connection between two essentials of the quantum world—the collapse of the wave function, and action at a distance or non-locality—to the presence of Emerson's universal consciousness, or Over-Soul. It seems clear, however, that such a case has been plausibly, if not yet empirically, made by a number of scientists and those who report their theories. Proof, as we understand that term, may not be too distant.

One example of the current state of modern physics and the public's growing interest in various theories is Brian Greene's *The Fabric of the Cosmos.* Greene is a professor of physics and mathematics at Columbia University and is one of the more reflective professionals in his willingness to enter the public arena to explore various theories of the nature of the universe. In the book's final chapter, he speculates on the possibility, entertained by a number of physicists, that space/time itself may be an illusion. Without fully making that assertion himself, he does say, "space and time may similarly dissolve when scrutinized with the most fundamental formulation of nature's laws." Since human beings are part of the fabric of space/time, where does that leave our understanding of matter and the world we take to be real?

Any assertion that space/time is illusory naturally leaves us with the possibility that what is fundamental, i.e., reality itself, must then be defined in terms other than material. What those other terms might be has long been expressed by the idealists as mind, or consciousness. But Greene does not, or will not, take that leap, although others have. He does say, however, that "rumors of space/time's impending departure from deep physical law are not born of zany theorizing." This remark constitutes a concession from the physics establishment and could not have been imagined a generation ago.

Although Greene does not suggest what the nature of reality might be if it is not based on space/time, others have shown less hesitancy in doing so. One of the most important of such physicists is Roger Penrose, Emeritus Professor of Mathematics at Oxford University and former teacher of Stephen Hawking. The two have worked together many times to provide the world with a deeper understanding of the universe. Penrose's magnum opus, *The Road to Reality* concludes with speculations about the fundamental nature of reality. Although Penrose declares the holy grail of a unified theory of reality is probably many years away, he does offer his own view of reality in the book's final chapter.

For Penrose, reality must be made up of three related and interactive components: physical space/time, mentality (or consciousness) and Platonic absolutes. As to the role of consciousness in this triad, he makes the following point:

> Any universe that can 'be observed' must, as a logical necessity, be capable of supporting conscious mentality, since consciousness is precisely what plays the ultimate role of 'observer.' This fundamental requirement could well provide constraints of the universe's physical laws, or physical parameters, in order that conscious mentality can (and will) exist.

Certainly this observation, if accurate, places consciousness (the fundamental ground of being in Idealism) at the center of the question of reality and suggests strongly that those materialists who scoff at the notion of consciousness existing outside the activity of the human brain, have to revise their definitions of matter *and* reality. Penrose also makes the significant observation that what we call consciousness "must be a real physical process, arising 'out there' in the physical world."

These speculations by practicing physicists, rather than science writers who interpolate from the work of the professionals, present us with the kind of solid grounding that materialists insist upon before they will accept theoretical assertions. The effect has been to seriously challenge the materialist view of the universe with its definition of reality as grounded in matter. The reign of matter is in serious jeopardy and with it, the prevalent view of a limited consciousness.

Naturally, the question of consciousness, its nature and source, is much debated and no single theory has been accepted. Indeed, at this writing, Amazon lists more than 3,800 books dealing directly or indirectly with the subject of consciousness, leaving the field wide open. Although most of these books lead from a materialist basis and assume that all consciousness derives from brain function and is therefore an epiphenomenon of evolution, other approaches are being advanced in greater numbers.

In the light of our present concern to listen to Emerson in our own space/time, the most comparable work has been that of Amit Goswami, a theoretical physicist and member of the faculty at the University of Oregon Institute of Theoretical Physics. His book *The Self-Aware Universe* takes the argument further by declaring unequivocally that consciousness is in fact the ground state of the universe, and he presents powerful arguments to support his conclusions.

Goswami's primary argument begins with the data collected by the famous double slit experiments showing that human observation (i.e., consciousness) causes the collapse of the wave function, creating particle/wave ambiguity and demonstrating the principle that consciousness and matter are fundamentally entangled, and that without the participation of consciousness, matter would not exist at all, or at best would not assemble into something tangible. Goswami, who also weaves Advaita Vedanta, the Indian philosophy of non-duality, into his explanations, refers to his views as the Monist Idealism Interpretation of Quantum Mechanics.

Philosophers and scientists have been speculating for years now about the question of the relationship between consciousness and matter. They raise questions such as, "Does the tree in the forest, or the forest itself, exist at all if there is no one there to see it?" Goswami's answer to such questions is that of course the forest exists, because universal consciousness is there not only to "see" it, as it were, but to participate in its very existence. One does not need what we think of as "ordinary" human consciousness to be in attendance.

The essential message here is that *consciousness is not in us; we are in it,* and the human mind is a faculty of that pervasive and permeating consciousness, just as William James asserted when speaking of the same forest that "our individuality builds but accidental fences" in that greater consciousness. This assertion suggests that a pervasive consciousness participates in species development, and that what we call human brain consciousness is a reflection of this greater, more pervasive consciousness required by what Penrose calls a "real physical process."

Debates among materialists and idealists will continue as long as there is doubt about the true nature of consciousness and its relation to matter. Materialists take the easier empirical way and insist that the observer in quantum effects is not the same as consciousness, that consciousness is strictly electro-chemical brain function. The question, of course, is, What do we mean by observation? Materialists such as physicist Steven Weinberg insist that consciousness (human at least) is an epiphenomenon, merely a product of evolutionary development and not a necessary fact of nature. Idealists see this position as the Custer's Last Stand of materialist thinking.

Goswami, for example, makes this observation in *The Self-Aware Universe:*

"The more the universe seems comprehensible, the more it seems meaningless," said Nobel laureate physicist Steven Weinberg at the end of his popular book on cosmology. We agree, concepts such as nonlocal and unitive consciousness and the idea of nonlocal collapse make the universe less comprehensible to the materialist scientist. These concepts also make the universe a lot more meaningful to everyone else.

The questions are: To what degree is universal consciousness also entangled with matter and also how is it connected in some way to normal human consciousness? And, most important, what difference does it make to our lives, and in the way we see and respond to the world? The answers depend first on the distinctions we make in sorting out the various faculties of the human mind. Emerson wrote in his journal, "What is life but what a man is thinking of all day." The human brain is busy absorbing sensory data in millions of bits each second and then sifting that data into useless and useful information. In addition, we think about daily problems while the mind is doing its sifting and we are also engaged, on occasion, in creative thought. We also know now that a hidden layer of consciousness (the "unconscious") lies beneath the surface of awareness and is also sifting data and motivating our actions. In the midst of all this activity, Emerson suggests, there is also the influx of a greater consciousness which permeates everything with its laws and influx of subtle influence. What does the New Physics say about all this?

Another physicist, Paul Davies, in his book *The Mind of God*, makes the intriguing observation that the human mind seems remarkably attuned to the subtlety and complexity of what he refers to as "the cosmic code," that is, the set of laws that govern the operations of the universe. Assuming as he does that human consciousness is derived from biological evolution, Davies is therefore puzzled by our ability to create and master the mathematics necessary to penetrate the mysteries of the macro- and microcosms of the universe. Since in evolutionary terms our survival does not seem to require those kinds of skills, where then does this ability come from? If we are able to intuit laws having nothing to do with our own survival and self-interest, perhaps these laws are wired into our thinking processes. For example, if life on this planet becomes endangered before the human race becomes extinct, we may be equipped with the intelligence to plan an exit to another home in the galaxy.

Davies goes on to explore the nature of mathematics as the science and art of penetrating these great mysteries. He concludes that these laws are really expressive of reality in the Platonic sense, and that mathematical laws are not merely constructs of the human mind to explain things, but are rather Platonic ideas at the core of reality and that human genius has been able to uncover them and will continue to do so in the future. This conclusion draws very near to the Perennial Philosophy and the notion that consciousness is universally pervasive and that the laws are contained within it.

As Emerson explains in "The Transcendentalist," his essay on this topic, the above assertion can be credited in part to Kant, who argued that the human mind is in itself a model of the universe. Such a relationship between our mind and the universe would account for why human beings like Einstein can uncover these laws in the first place. Emerson articulated the same principle in "The Natural History of the Intellect" when he wrote, "Leaving aside the question which was prior, egg or bird, I believe the mind is the creator of the world, and is ever creating; —that at last Matter is dead Mind; that mind makes the senses it sees with; that the genius of man is a continuation of the power that made him and that has not done making him." If we actually listen to that, where does it take us? Where did it take Einstein?

Einstein also believed the human mind fundamentally equipped to grasp the laws of the universe. He put it this way: "I hold it true that pure thought can grasp reality, as the Ancients dreamed. We can discover by means of purely mathematical constructions the concepts and the laws connecting them with each other, which furnish the key to the understanding of natural phenomena." This assertion is much debated today because a Theory of Everything cannot presently be experimentally tested. This fact divides the physics community into those who demand experimental verification and those who are comfortable with a mathematical construct, particularly if it is elegant and contains within its framework the known laws of how things work.

Emerson would have agreed with the theorists. His reason for such a conclusion, however, was informed by the conviction that the human mind is a microcosm of the universe itself, and that they both—the mind and the universe—operate by and through the same laws. Therefore, if we understand the human mind, we understand the universe and by extension, we know "the mind of God," as Einstein expressed it. Of the many examples of this principle in Emerson's writings, this passage from "The Transcendentalist" marks a special moment in his grasp of the principle:

> The idealist has another measure, which is metaphysical, namely, the rank which things themselves take in his consciousness; not at all, the size or appearance. Mind is the only reality, of which men and all other natures are better or worse reflectors. Nature, literature, history, are only subjective phenomena. . . . His thought, —that is the Universe. His experience inclines him to behold the procession of facts you call the world, as flowing perpetually outward from an invisible, unsounded centre in himself, centre alike of him and of them, and necessitating him to regard all things as having a subjective or relative existence, relative to that aforesaid Unknown Centre of him.

Emerson is, of course, speaking of himself as he describes the mind of the Idealist. The key phrase, "His thought, —that is the Universe" leaps from the page as an expression of unity. Wallace Stevens said, in an Emersonian outburst, that identity is the vanishing point of resemblance. The identity of Einstein's "pure thought" with the nature of the universe is the highest expression of human attainment. It places us in union with, not separate from, the laws of the universe—an idea which is related to but fundamentally different from the reductionist notion that we are merely made of the same "stuff."

This identity with the laws is the key to Transcendentalism and its compatibility with scientific understanding of nature. It also answers Davies' question about how human beings have managed to describe through mathematical abstraction the laws that govern both quantum reality and so-called "classical" reality. We are describing ourselves, as well as God. Emerson put it best when he said in his journal for December, 1833. "The best we can say of God, we mean of the mind as it is known to us."

Davies is not as ready as others have been to equate consciousness and reality or to make the statement that mind *is* reality, or that, as Emerson posited, human beings participate in a specific reality called Universal Mind, such that our individual minds are part and parcel of that greater Mind. The essay "History" begins with the provocative sentence, "There is one mind common to all individual men." Emerson's meaning here is just this identity of Mind and reality and is not the same in kind as Jung's idea of the Collective Unconscious. History, for Emerson, is the account of the activity of this universal mind.

Therefore, when Emerson speaks of mind in this way, he is thinking of this higher mind. He is also not speaking directly of the creative imagination, at least not in its limited or circumscribed sense of the ordinary faculties of mind that modernism seeks to limit to biological brain activity. Emerson's definition of mind seeks to include the evidences of great genius, the ability of savants, the unexplained examples of creative genius in the arts, in mathematics, in language, and in physics which have startled us through the ages.

Now, if we consider the evidences of the physicists and their carefully framed conclusions—derived from genius in the form of pure thought, from experimentation and mathematical calculation—we can consider Emerson's most radical statement on the causes of creation and the ground state of the universe. It is a statement from *Nature* and it comes "from a certain poet." Some think the poet was his lifelong friend and neighbor Amos Bronson Alcott, whose own journal was full of startling images and spiritual revelation. Others think the passage comes from Emerson's own intuitive influx, influenced by texts from the Perennial Philosophy. In any case, it presents as clearly as anything else in the nineteenth century a theory of consciousness as the ground state of the universe.

> 'Man is the dwarf of himself. Once he was permeated and dissolved by spirit. He filled nature with his overflowing currents. Out from him sprang the sun and moon; from man, the sun; from woman, the moon. The laws of his mind, the periods of his actions externized themselves into day and night, into the year and the seasons. But, having made for himself this huge shell, his waters retired; he no longer fills the veins and veinlets; he is shrunk to a drop. He sees, that the structure still fits him, but fits him colossally. Say, rather, once it fitted him, now it corresponds to him from far and on high. He adores timidly his own work. Now is man the follower of the sun, and woman the follower of the moon. Yet sometimes he starts in his slumber, and wonders at himself and his house, and muses strangely at the resemblance betwixt him and it. He perceives that if his law is still paramount, if still he have elemental power, if his word is sterling yet in nature, it is not conscious power, it is not inferior but superior to his will. It is Instinct.' Thus my Orphic poet sang.

"Out from him . . ." How else can we interpret this passage except as an identity with the presence of consciousness in the universe? It does not suggest that human beings in some earlier state created the heavens and earth, as God is described as doing in Genesis. It does suggest, however, that universal consciousness was the causal force in the cosmic dance which created the universe. As the result of the loss of elemental unity, human beings lost this connection and we have become mere followers, all as a result of becoming alienated from our source.

Seeing this passage in this way and knowing the support Emerson received from ancient sources, it is not difficult to reverse the progression and to read the pagan myths in this new light. Rather than see them as imaginative human explanations for nature's causes and effects, it is possible to see these myths as revelatory influxes from a *logos* or universal consciousness central to the creation. And certainly the work of mythologists such as Jung, Kerenyi, and Campbell posit a much closer connection for so-called primitive peoples to these same universal forces. Emerson knew the power of myth and said about it, ". . . the legend is tossed from believer to poet, from poet to believer, everybody adding a grace or dropping a fault or rounding the form, until it gets an ideal truth." He might just as easily have been describing the mathematics of quantum mechanics as the visions of early native peoples or the Greek naturalists in 500 B.C.E.

Recall, Emerson said in *Nature*, "Undoubtedly we have no questions to ask which are unanswerable. We must trust the perfection of the creation so far, as to believe that whatever curiosity the order of things has awakened in our minds, the order of things can satisfy." And as I am fond of saying about Emerson, it does well to take him seriously, to examine his work as if he meant what he said, because he might have. Too many readers of Emerson read him too metaphorically, as a Romantic veering off into flights of fancy to elicit dreams of grandeur. The effect of this latter view reduces his language to protean vagaries.

The naturalist in Emerson means it when he says that the order of things—the laws of the universe—both awaken our curiosity and satisfy it as well. In that regard, what then is extraordinary genius? Is it just the result of a larger brain or greater intelligence? Or, perhaps, is it an infusion of power from the source that permeates all of space/time, but one still abiding by the rule of sufficiency? Emerson felt that ordinary people, like us, had barely enough reserves of strength and perception to survive ordinary living, much less devote time to answering metaphysical questions. We possess just enough conscious awareness to get us through the day, but no more. And yet, perhaps we have more capacity than we imagine. Or, perhaps it's best that true genius is so rare.

A related view, more Eastern in origin, sees the phenomenon of genius as evidence of reincarnation, the transmigration of a soul from one embodiment to another, bringing with it many lifetimes of development, including genius in a particular field. The belief is that the soul retains sensory impressions and karmic debt from previous lifetimes, which in turn must be paid in subsequent lifetimes. Further, the theory holds that the subtle substances of soul migrate after death to like substances and find their way to new birth. In this way it is possible for genius to appear in very young persons who exhibit extraordinary abilities and accomplishments.

Davies explores this view by recounting an instance of unexplained genius in the great Indian mathematician Ramanujan (1887–1920), an untrained and barely educated Brahmin who was born in Erode, a small village south of Madras. Unable to gain admission to the university because he was both poor and unprepared in required subjects, he nonetheless excelled in mathematics, particularly the theory of numbers. He eventually attracted the attention of G.H. Hardy, a famous mathematician at Cambridge University, who, according to Davies, was astounded by Ramanujan's considerable skills. Davies goes on to say that no one understood how this poor Indian, without any formal training, achieved such long-lasting and significant work, including more than three thousand significant formulas. Many in India naturally attributed the phenomenal results of Ramanujan's genius to reincarnation, offering his life and work as proof positive of the transmigration of souls.

For Emerson's part, the idea of reincarnation found expression in several places—most clearly and importantly in a passage from "Fate."

> The revelation of Thought takes man out of servitude into freedom. We rightly say of ourselves, we were born, and afterward we were born again, and many times. We have successive experiences so important, that the new forgets the old, and hence the mythology of the seven or the nine heavens. The day of days, the great day of the feast of life, is that in which the inward eye opens to the Unity in things, to the omnipresence of law; —sees that what is must be, and ought to be, or is the best. This beatitude dips from on high down on us, and we see.

It is not in us so much as we are in it. If the air come to our lungs, we breathe and live; if not, we die. If the light come to our eyes, we see; else not. And if truth come to our mind, we suddenly expand to its dimensions, as if we grew to worlds. We are as lawgivers; we speak for Nature; we prophesy and divine.

Being spiritually "born again" in this lifetime is, of course, the basis of evangelical Christianity, its core spiritual experience. Emerson no doubt has this meaning in mind as well in this passage. He said in a journal entry in 1859, "On that bright moment when we are born into thought, we are instantaneously uplifted out of the rank we had." For some more cautious souls, these images represent various psychological states, levels of self-awareness, or new stages of intellectual development. For others of a more spiritual turn of mind, the descriptions of various states of awareness are steps towards enlightenment, of achieving higher and higher levels of spiritual knowledge and being. For Emerson, tempting as they were to examine in this way, these distinctions were irrelevant, more like evidence of spiritual materialism. His experience with the world had given him a firmer grip on reality.

In his poem "Brahma," Emerson expresses his debt to Eastern philosophy through a series of mythopoetic images. The poem recapitulates *Nature*, establishing unity rather than duality and making reference to the sacred Seven, probably a reference to the seven major gods of the Vedic tradition. But the main thrust of the poem is found in stanza two, as polarities are collapsed into unity, just as the old gods became one in Brahma. The last verse shatters the duality of heaven and earth and establishes a new paradigm. Emerson is explicit in the matter when he writes,

> The strong gods pine for my abode,
> And pine in vain the sacred Seven;
> But thou, meek lover of the good!
> Find me, and turn thy back on heaven.

In the poem Emerson has taken another long leap into daring territory by asserting his own identity with the Over-Soul and writing from a stance that combines occult transmission with personal instruction to his readers. In other words, he brashly asserts that he is Brahma here. The key to his personal evocation of universal mind finds expression in the last line. Find the unity, he asserts, and turn your back on the dualistic religious imagery of earth and heaven, this world and that other, and then begin to see the unity, the one world in which self-recovery is possible.

Turning one's back on heaven also implies finding a theory of nature—or the world—that unifies all forms of experience and satisfies the longing for transcendence. One thinks, for example, of Robert Browning's dualism when he wrote, "A man's reach should exceed his grasp,/Or what's a heaven for?" Emerson would retort, "There is no other world; here or nowhere is the whole fact." His project was to fuse the notions of reach and grasp without a traditional myth of heaven as some aspiration of perfection and bliss.

In the Introduction to *Nature,* Emerson makes it clear that as an aspiring naturalist he will honor the observable facts of the universe and seek to discover its laws. "All science has one aim, namely, to find a theory of nature." The quest began among the ancients, reached a high point with Newton's laws and would next find new theories with the laws of Maxwell and the theories of Darwin in the nineteenth century. Emerson's glimpses into these realms of science made it a straightforward process to begin in familiar territory and work up into higher, spiritual laws.

From the beginning, Emerson's sole purpose was to reconcile science and metaphysics, to do what Aristotle failed to do because he became possessed with categorizing things. In order to accomplish his aim, Emerson had to transform a traditional view of Soul to higher consciousness and then to identify it as the ground of being. Therefore, after affirming the role of science in his thesis, he moves ahead to philosophy, declaring, "Philosophically considered, the universe is composed of Nature and the Soul." He then makes a declaration which allows him entry into transcendental ground by declaring that what he calls the NOT ME is Nature, including his own body and the rest of the universe of matter, or dead mind. What constitutes the ME is included in Soul and is distinct, eternal, and infinite. His next task, and this was a huge enterprise, was to eliminate the duality inherent in that proposition and to find the unity.

He departs from standard scientific procedure, as Einstein did after him, by declaring, "Whenever a true theory appears, it will be its own evidence." At a certain point in the effort to uncover universal laws, the application of empirical proofs has to be temporarily abandoned, just as it is now among the theoretical physicists. Presently, we are operating in that sphere with the controversial String Theory. The high energies necessary to prove String Theory cannot be achieved; therefore, there is no way to test String Theory. The theorists argue, however, that if the mathematics finally resolves the split between Relativity and Quantum Mechanics, we will have arrived at a "true" theory. In other words, mathematical elegance will be its own evidence, and there will be no need to prove it true experimentally. The theory will be its own evidence.

This exploration into the complexities of modern physics begs the question of what connection and eventual impact might a "theory of everything" have on our theme of the Dream of America? The unity that Emerson seeks throughout his work asks us to "turn our back on heaven" and look to Earth as our home and our unity as human beings with the cosmos. Indeed, heaven can and will wait. Our responsibility is to our home and its future, but to arrive at that realization we have to start at the beginning, to arrive at the unity within nature itself, where we began. Emerson's insight that the laws of the mind and the laws of the universe are one and the same tells us where, in fact, to begin.

When Einstein wondered what it is about the human mind that allows us to arrive at the mathematical formulas describing the inner workings of the universe, he already knew the answer. The laws are the same. And since the laws are the same, it means that as we care for our individual minds and the body that supports its life, so too we take care of the earth in the same way. Just as we treat a fever in the body, we must also treat the fever in the earth, seeking its cause and treating it by taking responsibility as we would care for a feverish child. It is a unity, not an either/or. This unity is the core of Idealism.

The coming decades will reveal whether or not the Idealist vision of reality has credence. If it does, the impacts will loom much larger than just for our own individual knowledge and understanding. The nation, too, will benefit as these facts impact decisions about how we invest our treasure and how that investment impacts individual lives. If a deeper understanding of our significant place in the cosmos emerges, individual human life itself will achieve greater value and fewer lives will be lost in futile wars and senseless violence. The treasure that is life will find new respect. It will be, as we see next, the condition of sanity.

# 8

# The Condition of Sanity

AND yet there seems no need to fear that we should grow too wise. The path of truth has obstacles enough of its own. We dwell on the surface of nature. We dwell amidst surfaces; and surface laps so closely on surface, that we cannot easily pierce to see the interior organism. Then the subtlety of things! Under every cause, another cause. Truth soars too high or dives too deep, for the most resolute inquirer. See of how much we know nothing.

RWE, "The Senses and the Soul"

Emerson taught throughout that the path to the formation of character is steep and narrow, but nonetheless is our essential business. As he said in a journal entry for 1845, "I am here to be worked upon." Few seem inclined to undertake the climb, and yet in these times, it appears more necessary and vital than ever because the ground beneath our feet trembles and the water is rising. How are we seriously to cope, to find a firm place to stand unless we undertake the one serious path to the ground of being? In addition to the term "self-recovery," Emerson referred to this work in "Self-Reliance" as achieving "the erect position."

When the New England Transcendentalists, with Emerson as their undeclared leader, undertook to publish the journal *Dial,* their organ of communication to a skeptical world, Emerson wrote for the 1842 edition a compassionate essay entitled "The Senses and the Soul." The passage above was followed by this reservation on the merits of the examined life:

> Our ignorance is great enough, and yet the fact most surprising is not our ignorance, but the aversation [aversion] of men from knowledge. That which, one would say, would unite all minds and join all hands, the ambition to push as far as fate would permit, the planted garden of man on every hand into the kingdom of Night, really fires the heart of few and solitary men. Tell men to study themselves, and for the most part, they find nothing less interesting.

There are at least two reasons why we don't make more progress in understanding the world through understanding ourselves: Things are too subtle and we find introspection too circular. It feels much more productive to move along a straight line, to follow a path on the surface of things, where we can experience and measure success. The trouble with surface-dwelling, however, is that one day we find ourselves nearing the end of life and, looking back, we find everything an indistinct blur. "What happened to my life?" we ask and with good reason. As that persistent gad-fly Socrates told us, the unexamined life is not worth having. Deep down we know that to be true because the experience of surfaces confirms it. As Emerson put it, we live in deep prisons of our own making and when we seek to break free, we haven't the tools to force the prison door.

Like Jung in the next century, Emerson saw self-recovery as the process of soul-making, and it involved awakening to the full potential of human life, and again, he called it "the infinitude of the private man." (See Appendix II for passages on the subject of the Examined Life). Those in his circle, especially Alcott, Thoreau, and Margaret Fuller, were equally devoted to the examined life and to ways in which this awakening might actually take place. How to do so was an earnest debate among them.

Emerson was no fool and understood the difficulties involved. First, we are so confident of our certainties, so careless of our experience, that we pass through life dazzled by our sense impressions and satisfied with glittering surfaces. Emerson's Intellect in us remains as if drugged asleep by the whir of images in space and time, and we are content to let the world have its way with us. But then, when it finally does, when fate rises up in our face and we are unprepared, the shock is all too often greater than we can bear, and we are shattered into pieces, when all it would require to take our lives back again is to find a firm place to plant our feet. We need a point of observation, that higher platform above the floods of experience.

We begin, as always with Emerson, with idealism, with encouragement, only later refining the principle with the pragmatic concerns of accomplishment. In the final chapter of *Nature,* entitled "Prospects," we receive the principle of self-recovery:

> But the best read naturalist who lends an entire and devout attention to truth, will see that there remains much to learn of his relation to the world, and that it is not to be learned by any addition or subtraction or other comparison of known quantities, but is arrived at by untaught sallies of the spirit, by a continual self-recovery, and by entire humility. He will perceive that there are far more excellent qualities in the student than preciseness and infallibility; that a guess is often more fruitful than an indisputable affirmation, and that a dream may let us deeper into the secret of nature than a hundred concerted experiments.

The task of self-recovery begins with observation of and participation in the natural world and then moves, with the intuitive faculty, into more interior insights. These "untaught sallies of the spirit" lead us away from the world's *tuitions* into the spirit's *intuitions.* Formal education (tuition) takes us only so far, that is, into the world of order and classifications, into the gifts of language and reason. The next, more challenging step, is to trust that the mysteries will reveal the underlying truths of the laws of nature.

Listening further, we learn from "The Natural History of the Intellect" how this process is meant to work:

> The condition of sanity is to respect the order of the intellectual world; to keep down talent in its place, to enthrone the instinct. There must be perpetual rallying and self-recovery. Each talent is ambitious and self-asserting; it works for show and for the shop, and the greater it grows the more is the mischief and the misleading, so that presently all is wrong.

A deeper glimpse into the process reveals the discomforting step of needing to "keep down talent." As we learned in "Spiritual Laws," talent leads us to our proper expression and a sound place among the rest of humanity. Developing natural talent leads us properly into the world. But Emerson warns against *enthroning* talent as the highest of our attributes rather than putting instinct first. All we have to do is watch the results of worldly fame upon the character of individuals of talent to see the danger. We can easily identify with talent rather than employ it in a measured way.

The world shows us daily the results of placing talent first: writers who glory in expression without substance; athletes who squander ability by not being able to perform when it really matters; musicians with consummate skill but no instinct for the soul of music. Placing instinct first, however, leads talent into the arena where genius can flourish.

Once the principle of self-recovery is understood and practiced in the life, the individual is prepared for whatever life presents. And in these times, having a place to stand is crucial, especially when all so-called truths are called into question. In "Circles," Emerson completes the thought:

Valor consists in the power of self-recovery, so that a man cannot have his flank turned, cannot be out-generalled, but put him where you will, he stands. This can only be by his preferring truth to his past apprehension of truth; and his alert acceptance of it, from whatever quarter; the intrepid conviction that his laws, his relations to society, his Christianity, his world, may at any time be superseded and decease.

This last reflection, the reference to *his* Christianity, speaks to self reliance in matters of personal faith and is perhaps the most personal of his observations on the principle of self-recovery. Emerson had to stand firm not to be "out-generalled" by the powers of the doctrinal authorities of his time. At the same time, however, even more significant for him was the constant process of revision as he grew in knowledge and insight and his refusal to be locked in to a position that at some later time might have to be revised. The question becomes how are we to penetrate to the strictest truth, to know that we have finally found our place to stand.

An example of the process of such strict clarification comes in the great essay "Experience." The essay was written in 1844, two years after the sudden death of Ralph Waldo, Jr., at age five. This loss of his son severely tested Emerson's resolve to reach confidently into the heart of reality and away from the deadening repose of a dream world. As he said at the outset, "Ghostlike we glide through nature, and should not know our place again." But he was determined to look squarely at this experience, feeling fully, testifying accurately, and writing truthfully.

In the following passage from the beginning of the essay, Emerson reflects on the nature of loss and its meaning. Be warned, the language is severe. Even shocking in its honesty.

People grieve and bemoan themselves, but it is not half so bad with them as they say. There are moods in which we court suffering, in the hope that here, at least, we shall find reality, sharp peaks and edges of truth. But it turns out to be scene-painting and counterfeit. The only thing grief has taught me, is to know how shallow it is. That, like all the rest, plays about the surface, and never introduces me into the reality, for contact with which, we would even pay the costly price of sons and lovers. Was it Boscovich who found out that bodies never come in contact? Well, souls never touch their objects. An innavigable sea washes with silent waves between us and the things we aim at and converse with. Grief too will make us idealists. In the death of my son, now more than two years ago, I seem to have lost a beautiful estate, —no more.

Sometimes the truth is harsh. Obsessed by loss, we lose the edge of truth because our focus, our emotional life, becomes possessed by the ghosts of the departed. The universe seems all about gain, change, and loss, in the rhythms of birth, existence, and death, as change "plays about the surface" and prevents us from penetrating to something deeper, to a place, perhaps, where the soul does finally touch its object. Fifteen years after the death of Emerson's son, the town of Concord opened a new cemetery, Sleepy Hollow, and Emerson had his son's coffin exhumed and moved to the new family plot, where he himself would be buried in 1882. Before little Waldo's coffin was placed in the ground, Emerson pried open the lid and looked at the remains. Morbid curiosity? No. Change, decay, transformation, all these help to clarify whatever it is that remains permanent, whatever we are meant to focus our attention upon. Too much "reality," you say? For us, in this antiseptic age, I say hardly enough.

Ordinary experience deceives with its seeming importance at every turn. We do indeed live mechanically, asleep, harnessed to habitual thinking and action. In the midst of such illusion, the observant "I" has little chance to see things clearly. So possessed are we by illusion that we barely touch the world truly as we move through it. The stars blink overhead but we scarcely look up to see our birthplace. The air smells of fall or the coming of snow, yet we are surprised by the "sudden" change of weather. Emerson explains this neglect as caused by the "evanescence and lubricity," of nature, its tendency to thwart our attentions, to keep us focused on forms. When Heraclitus said, "Nature loves to hide," he spoke directly to the difficulty of lifting the veil of her secrets. Again, this passage from "Experience":

> I take this evanescence and lubricity of all objects, which lets them slip through our fingers then when we clutch hardest, to be the most unhandsome part of our condition. Nature does not like to be observed, and likes that we should be her fools and playmates. We may have the sphere for our cricket-ball, but not a berry for our philosophy. Direct strokes she never gave us power to make; all our blows glance, all our hits are accidents. Our relations to each other are oblique and casual.

There is longing in this passage. Sadly, "oblique and casual" is the human condition without philosophy. If this condition is "the most unhandsome" part of our nature, where is our recovery? What hope have we to penetrate, to overcome these limitations? Here is Emerson's connection to the work of Gurdjieff and Ouspensky, whose insights into human limitation confirm Emerson's harsh observations. If our minds are locked into mechanical patterns of habitual reaction to experience, what can we do? Their techniques surrounding "the work" propose rigorous physical and psychological exercises designed to break down the habitual patterns that program our existence, to penetrate those patterns and elevate conscious awareness. Then and only then can the observant "I" take its place in relation to experience to allow us a modicum of self-recovery.

More than most, Emerson understood how difficult this process is. As he put it, "Of what use to make heroic vows of amendment if the same old law-breaker is to keep them?" The problem is that the "old law-breaker" is too often in control. Resolve is one thing, habit another. The edge of practice is too often dulled by the vague and slow appearance of reward. How are we expected to reform when the promise of reality refuses to reveal itself like a revelation or a lightning strike? We can't live with such subtlety. We are impatient. If I practice my scales, why can't I play the *Polonaise?*

However, what is our practical choice in the matter? If we allow ourselves to be creatures of this fleeting, doubtful world, we end by living in duality, in variety, in chaos. Since these patterns of behavior are what constitute reality most of the time, experience teaches us to take sides against all sorts of illusory enemies. Finding the still point in all this turbulence seems momentary, ephemeral, and then we have to get on with the conflict, with the duality of life. A friend said recently that she found stillness in her yoga class but then she was off and running a minute later, caught up again in the whirling world. The reality is that the world is still enough; it is the mind that does the whirling. But the effort to find the still point is worth the attention, especially if the ground thus arrived at gives us a firm ground of being on which to make our stand on the slippery surfaces of things. The longer we watch, the better chance we have of finding an anchor that eventually holds in the shifting sand.

We may, as Emerson says, be born to a unity, but the particular draws our attention and leaves us fragmented. How, then, can we grasp the intuitions of reality? What are the symbols that communicate a sense of the essence of it? "Experience" explains.

> The baffled intellect must still kneel before this cause, which refuses to be named, —ineffable cause, which every fine genius has essayed to represent by some emphatic symbol, as, Thales by water, Anaximenes by air, Anaxagoras by (Nous) thought, Zoroaster by fire, Jesus and the moderns by love: and the metaphor of each has become a national religion. The Chinese Mencius has not been the least successful in his generalization. "I fully understand language," he said, "and nourish well my vast-flowing vigor." — "I beg to ask what you call vast-flowing vigor?" —said his companion. "The explanation," replied Mencius, "is difficult. This vigor is supremely great, and in the highest degree unbending. Nourish it correctly, and do it no injury, and it will fill

up the vacancy between heaven and earth. This vigor accords with and assists justice and reason, and leaves no hunger." —In our more correct writing, we give to this generalization the name of Being, and thereby confess that we have arrived as far as we can go. Suffice it for the joy of the universe, that we have not arrived at a wall, but at interminable oceans.

The name we give—Being, God, Absolute, Infinite, Over-Soul, Universal Mind, Bergson's *élan vital*, or the Vast-Flowing Vigor of Mencius—is the way we circle and eventually contain the lubricity of the subject. In our "more correct writing" 'Being' is the evasion we prefer. But all these terms express the Ideal vision of what lies at the heart of the interminable ocean of reality. But be aware that our individual vision is disfigured by the connotations of the symbolism and the complexities of historical distortion. As Emerson affirms, we have arrived as far as we can go. We have to beware of illusory resonances and premature satisfactions, both of which can deflect us in our journeying on the pathless path.

What Emersonian language supplies us for our search is depth, balance, and patience for the long journey—and, it must be said, enough ambiguity to keep us from settling too soon for those attractive premature satisfactions. His early idealism is balanced by a later realism, an early instinct for soaring eloquence balanced by a later preference for a more muscular excavation. "Experience" is, on balance, a serious, reflective essay, somber in tone, and yet encouraging when it says things like, "There never was a right endeavor but it succeeded. Patience and patience, we will win at last." And then, he turns and reflects on the nature of the Fall, that historic unhandsome myth still living in our innermost awareness.

It is very unhappy, but too late to be helped, the discovery we have made, that we exist. That discovery is called the Fall of Man. Ever afterwards, we suspect our instruments. We have learned that we do not see directly, but mediately, and that we have no means of correcting these colored and distorting lenses which we are, or of computing the amount of their errors. Perhaps these subject-lenses have a creative power; perhaps there are no objects. Once we lived in what we saw; now, the rapaciousness of this new power, which threatens to absorb all things, engages us.

Here is Emerson on the topic of the observing "I," that newly arrived evolutionary faculty, that modern differentiation that tells us that we exist, that makes us existentially self-aware. This unique consciousness arrived, we are told, when around the primitive campfire, one hunter turned to another, surprised, and said, "We're talking!" It is an unhappy development only in the sense that it separates us from the ground, the innocent communal fire, and interposes doubt where once there was harmony, and quite naturally we feel that loss deeply. Self-consciousness is what separates us from ourselves and the world and causes existential despair and loneliness. But it is also the source of knowledge and the origin of our unique consciousness. It is the gift that takes us away from the fire into the expanding universe.

When Emerson says that "once we lived in what we saw," he describes a former state of innocence, of existing amid surfaces in what Thomas Mann described in his great novella *Tonio Kröger* as the bliss of the commonplace. Emerson describes its opposite, this our new state, as rapacious, a devouring hunger for understanding and meaning brought on by the doubt and longing of our new condition. But he is certainly correct to say that it is too late to change the fact of our separation from the surfaces of things. A return to innocence has to be considered as a failure of imagination and a terrible self-deception.

The startling fact is that meaning and consciousness feel the same. We are said to be fully conscious of something when we grasp its meaning. If, for example, an observer studies nature and its living constituents and becomes suddenly conscious of patterns and symmetries among and between species, where before there was only dissimilarity and randomness, he imbues nature with meaning and therefore becomes fully conscious of it. In that instant, nature itself becomes conscious as well because the observer is part of nature and no longer outside it. Therefore, consciousness cannot be outside of it either. The observer can no longer distinguish between his observational awareness and that same awareness he is observing. It is no longer a dual framework

Ordinary self-awareness, however—the knowledge of our own death, the awareness that we are distinct individuals—is not the same thing as philosophical self-awareness. This differentiation in the mind is what Emerson means by "the creative self," that is, the growing and expanding awareness which all-encompassing Nature supplies and which eventually gives to human beings their grasp of the infinite. So what are we to do with this attribute? Emerson knew full well that in his inland farming community of Concord, Massachusetts, so evocative of America as a whole, scholars were not held in high esteem. What is this kind of thinking worth, they asked? Better to make something the town needs. But Emerson held fast to his knowing.

> People disparage knowing and the intellectual life, and urge doing. I am very content with knowing, if only I could know. That is an august entertainment, and would suffice me a great while. To know a little, would be worth the expense of this world. I hear always the law of Adrastia, "that every soul which had acquired any truth, should be safe from harm until another period."

Emerson's value to philosophy lies in both his method and his language. Although his method was clearly circular, it was usefully an upward spiral rather than a closed circle. His thought spirals out from an insight to a broader apprehension. Spirals are useful because the advancing curve remains close to the circle below it, anchoring its progress. It is like the action of a spring, propelling us upwards when pressured by our own imposed weight. In "Experience" the spiraling argument is the question he poses at the outset: "Where do we find ourselves?" His answer fills out all the subtleties of the question while still leaving us room for our own discoveries. Quite literally, we find ourselves in this world, between birth and death and perched on the fine edge of knowing and doing. We also find ourselves by acknowledging the presence of the observing "I" in its journey to develop the attributes of self-trust. And finally, we find ourselves by seeking out the ground of being upon which to stand.

Emerson's language is, of course, uniquely and powerfully eloquent. The display of his eloquence is confusing to those who suppose that sweeping figures and rash-sounding statements betray a wild Romanticism disconnected from reality. When he says in the essay that a human being is "a golden impossibility," and that "the line he must walk is a hair's discretion," and that "the wise through excess of wisdom is made a fool," we see him struggling with his own gifts, trying to keep in check the rare and unique talent he possessed. His friends Thoreau and Alcott would despair at not having the creative gifts of their friend and patron. Even his readers grow suspect as his language soars, Icarus-like, too near the sun of knowledge and insight. And yet, when taken in the circumscribed twenty-page doses of the essays, Emerson is the model of artistic discretion. One attentive hour with his vision suffices for a year, and what he taught us was how to marshal our gifts and to stay patient. "Do the work," he admonishes. So be it. An essay sits before us to read and study.

Inevitably, inquiry into the nature of experience turns in on itself and is complicated by our self-conscious grasp of existence. Emerson's explorations of experience first drew the polarized conclusion that the world he lived in was not the world he thought. Idealism attempts to carry out an idea of the world, an idea conceived in thought. Materialism sees the world as it comes to our sensory doorstep and takes it to be real enough. One of the tasks of philosophy is to explore the nature of that "real enough" in order to determine whether or not these sensory faculties are worthy of conceiving of an idea of the world. In the process, doubt arises, and a natural result of that doubt is skepticism.

Skepticism can be healthy or paralyzing. In "Experience" Emerson deals frankly with the skeptic. "So many things are unsettled which it is of the first importance to settle, —and, pending their settlement, we will do as we do." In the mid-world that Emerson recommends and populates along with other seekers, some reserve is both necessary and sensible. He refers to our life as "a tent for a night," a flitting state, reminding us of the life of a May fly.

This "tent for a night" we call life can be better than a sleep and a dream by virtue of a healthy skepticism and a readiness not to accept the first attractive system we encounter. Our personal history often evolves in two opposing methods of influence. In religious matters, we are usually presented in our youth with a tradition fully articulated as worthy of devotion. At some later time, we begin to doubt, perhaps, and to develop a skeptical attitude as we mature in the tradition. At some point, we either reject early teachings altogether or we refine them into a more comfortable acceptance.

The opposite of this process takes place in any self-motivated exposure to philosophy. In this discipline, we are usually presented with a survey of ancient and modern thinkers presented not as fact or truth but as history. As a result, we defer taking sides in a philosophical debate between the materialists and the idealists. In this exercise, skepticism is natural and forms part of the substance of the final framework we select. In a real sense, academic instruction is based on skepticism. We are trained to be detached and not take sides.

Emerson was aware of the tensions of this debate. In a late lecture entitled "Life and Literature," delivered in 1861, he looked at the issue:

> The systems of philosophy are few, and repeat each other. They are all structural, and only express the necessities of the human mind. Thus, one affirms materialism, and mind is defined as only a highly rarefied or distilled form of matter, and this is pressed to absurd and immoral conclusions. Then a new reasoner exposes the flaws in the logic and the absurdity of the theory, and affirms the doctrine of idealism; proceeds to deny the existence of matter, and pours a contempt on the senses, and the sensuous life. For a time, this charms

the minds of men: all good thinkers turn their attention to it, until everything is thought of that can clear or verify the doctrine. When all the sense that offers has been said, then extravagant statements of the doctrine are made, until the minds of men are driven to the other side, and some middle ground, some eclecticism, is hit upon, not open to the extreme statements. And, in this way, we commonly say the four systems of Materialism, Idealism, Dogmatism, and Skepticism continually follow each other and reproduce each other like the four seasons round the year.

What Emerson is describing are the seasonal changes in our intellectual uncertainties, as we go from materialism (the conviction that only matter is existent), to idealism (in which we affirm the existence of mind as an entity, in conjunction with soul and spirit), to dogmatism (systems of a positive nature coupled with a sense of finality), to skepticism (which asserts the limitations of all knowledge and questions all propositions as doubtful). These seasonal changes leave us hot one minute and cold the next.

Certainly the human mind does have its "necessities," or fundamental needs, and both materialism and idealism fulfil those needs. Without recommending a movement towards eclecticism, Emerson describes the tendency to mix and match ideas and systems in order to arrive at something suitable for the times, in order to avoid theories of matter-only or spirit-only. His own journey (and here he is writing in his late fifties) saw the benefits of respecting matter while seeking spirit. One is reminded of Dr. Johnson's refutation of Bishop Berkeley's pure idealism by furiously kicking a rock to prove the reality of matter. One broken toe later, Johnson painfully reaffirmed his belief in materialism.

Such incidents argue strongly for a cooler, less painful approach. Emerson saw that the world, whatever its true nature, owed him nothing, that to claim otherwise was not only arrogant, but pointless. "I am thankful for small mercies. I compared notes with one of my friends who expects everything of the universe, and is disappointed when anything is less than the best, and I found that I begin at the other extreme, expecting nothing, and am always full of thanks for moderate goods." The challenge is to stay positive and upright while expecting little and then to be steady and reflective when the "goods" roll in, as they did for Emerson in later years.

When the honors and rewards begin to accumulate, what can we claim? This question raises another aspect of skepticism, which is its role in evaluating not just the thoughts of others but the results of our own efforts and successes. This from "Experience":

> The ardors of piety agree at last with the coldest skepticism, —that nothing is of us or our works, —that all is of God. Nature will not spare us the smallest leaf of laurel. All writing comes by the grace of God, and all doing and having. I would gladly be moral, and keep due metes and bounds, which I dearly love, and allow the most to the will of man, but I have set my heart on honesty in this chapter, and I can see nothing at last, in success or failure, than more or less of vital force supplied from the Eternal.

The crux, then, is that all vital force comes from sources hidden from us. We can claim nothing for our small egos, which would otherwise swell in false satisfactions given free rein. In all our relations, nothing is more offensive than being in the presence of such a claim. As Emerson said, "We like very well to be praised for our action, but our conscience says, 'Not unto us.'" And when we encounter those who propose solutions to the great metaphysical questions and for whom the word "skeptic" spells weakness, our best response is withdrawal. Continuing:

> When I converse with a profound mind, or if at any time being alone I have good thoughts, I do not at once arrive at satisfactions, as when, being thirsty, I drink water, or go to the fire, being cold: no! but I am at first apprised of my vicinity to a new and excellent region of

life . . . every insight from this realm of thought is felt as initial, and promises a sequel. I do not make it; I arrive there, and behold what was there already.

Finally, then, being cautioned, the mature individual finds the virtue and value of conscious reflection and puts into practice its methods and benefits. In the essay "Intellect," which we consider in the next chapter, Emerson places the act of reflection in its proper place in the process of self-recovery and thus of real sanity.

At last comes the era of reflection, when we not only observe, but take pains to observe; when we of set purpose sit down to consider an abstract truth; when we keep the mind's eye open, whilst we converse, whilst we read, whilst we act, intent to learn the secret law of some class of facts.

# 9
# A Call to the Nation

W E BEGAN this book with a query from Stanley Cavell and his concern about our failure as a culture to listen to Emerson, one of our founding thinkers. I would like to begin this late chapter considering "Fate," a pivotal document for Cavell as well, with his comment about this essay and its importance to what he calls the Emersonian enterprise.

> The essay "Fate" is perhaps Emerson's principal statement about the human condition of freedom, even about something Emerson calls the paradox that freedom is necessary; we might formulate this as the human fatedness to freedom. This comes to speaking of the human fatedness to thinking, since "Intellect annuls Fate. So far as man thinks, he is free. . . . The revelation of Thought takes man out of servitude into freedom."

By now, we must have a sense of what Emerson meant when he said that we know ourselves to be a party to our present estate. This is the true Fall of Man, this self-conscious falling away into separateness, of knowing both too much and not enough about who and what we are. It would seem that as we step warily into the new millennium, it is the former that should concern us. Popular science informs us every day that DNA is destiny. As I write, women with a faulty version of a certain gene are twice as susceptible to breast cancer than those with a healthy version of the same gene. But this is just the beginning of the genetic revolution. We are told that within a few decades we will have the ability to turn genes off and on, even to grow new limbs when we lose one, as our distant cousins the salamanders have done for millennia.

In this age of biological determinism we think less of the influential movement of planets than we do of fate in our cellular heritage. Yet, what the scientific establishment does not and cannot yet say is what influences and causes pulse in the other more or less than 35,000 genes in our genome and which can be attributed to intellect and genius and how many to transcendence. We must have genes for consciousness, even as current parlance suggests the presence of a "God gene," Dean Hamer's assertion that we are hard-wired for transcendence. How about genes for freedom and for self-consciousness? Or, perhaps, those who are awake philosophically are also possessed of a faulty gene. After all, genius and madness live close together in our nature. Who's crazy?

Ideas of fate and destiny change as culture, science, religion, and art change. Like any good philosopher, Emerson devoted a good deal of thought to the question of fate. Scholarship tells us that over a period between 1850–53 he wrote and rewrote his lecture on Fate for inclusion in his series entitled *Conduct of Life*. The lecture never satisfied him and perhaps never quite satisfied his audiences either. The version we have as an essay in *Conduct of Life* is the clearest and most comprehensive of the several versions we have. Like its subject, it sweeps a broad landscape from the abstract to the practical and, at least for this reader, gives the broadest understanding of Emerson's views on determinism, what Emerson called "limitation," and free will.

Exploring the question of determinism vs. free will in our lives is a central gateway into the world of philosophy. Most would agree, I think, that neither extreme represents an accurate description of life experience. Naturalism once taught that we are leaves caught in the tide. We may also suppose that we have conscious control of our destiny. And so it is with some anxiety that we hear Emerson say in his late lecture on fate, "Nothing befalls us that we do not invite." Is this an absolute statement, meant to explain accident, physical illness, life span, indeed all circumstances? Is this true for a country as well?

That section of the lecture begins with an equally disturbing declaration. "There are no contingencies." But before we can object too strenuously, Emerson qualifies: "The doctrine of Fate only masks the lesson of the immutability and universality of Law." The Law (capitalized in the text) trumps Fate, and Law also includes free will. Emerson insists upon the universality of the Law in all matters, conscious and material. And yet the ghost of contingency lurks in the shadows.

Emerson was quite conscious of the thin edge of existence that life on this planet entails. On his maiden journey across the Atlantic in 1833 he recorded in his journal the experience of a storm just out of Boston: "A long storm from the second morn of our departure consigned all the five passengers to the irremedial chagrins of the stateroom, to wit, nausea, darkness, unrest, uncleanness, harpy appetite and harpy feeding, the ugly sound of water in mine ears, anticipations of going to the bottom . . ." No contingencies? Well, we can say, he did choose to embark in the first place. And many years later, in 1850, when his good friend Margaret Fuller was drowned off Long Island in a hurricane "within sight of land, in fact within 60 rods [330 yards] of the shore . . ." Emerson would not have said that Fuller had "invited" her tragic death. But truth be told, she even had nightmares about the journey ending as it did.

Emerson appears to be following the time-honored view that "character is fate." "Your fate is what you do," he says in the lecture, "because first it is what you are." What appears an extreme view of taking responsibility for what befalls us in life is a corrective, the tendency human beings have for not taking responsibility, for not correcting those moments of inattention that result in accident, for not thinking before we speak As he said, ". . . if we will only be careful not to intrude and chatter, the least occasion and the domestic hour will be grand and fateful."

As we think of the nation in these same terms, how are we to think about the terrorist attack of 9/11? Many thoughtful people at the time and since have examined the role played by America in the world and asked if the country bears any responsibility for the attack. This query evokes anger and resentment among those who feel we were blameless. Consider for a moment, this comment from "Fate": "But let us honestly state the facts. Our America has a bad name for superficialness. Great men, great nations, have not been boasters and buffoons, but perceivers of the terror of life, and have manned themselves to face it." Where was our attention?

If indeed Emerson is right and superficialness is a national fault, we need to take the necessary steps to correct our character. The opposite of superficial is thoroughness and depth of knowledge and insight. Many observers have voiced the same criticism. Consider Richard Hofstadter's 1963 cultural analysis *Anti-Intellectualism in American Life,* and Susan Jacoby's *The American Age of Unreason,* published in 2009, in which she argues that our place in the world is directly the result of "a crisis of memory and knowledge."

Even if we accept the harsh view that we are responsible for what befalls us, there is nonetheless the pervasive myth that Destiny is a force beyond our control. Emerson's notes for the lecture contain such observations:

> Grey clouds, short days, moonless nights, a drowsy sense of being dragged easily somewhere by that locomotive, Destiny, which, never seen, we yet know must be hitched on to the cars wherein we sit, —that is all that appears in the dark months.

It is the "drowsy sense," similar in kind to repose, that creates this feeling of the pull of Destiny through the darkness. It is an example of how we would feel that loss of freedom if we were awake enough to think it through. In "Fate," Emerson addresses all of the subtleties that swing, pendulum-like through the rhythms of limitation and freedom.

That there is this oscillation at all is a function of our degree of awareness in the moment of action.

We will not be toyed with in this matter of fate and free will. If Emerson chooses, finally, to address the subject, he had better be straight with us and not coy or lean too far to the side of free will if that is not how the balance truly leans. Cavell thinks that Emerson chose to address the subject in 1850 because of the Fugitive Slave Law and the rising tide of public anger (finally) over slavery in America. It would be a brief decade before South and North, Slave and Free, came to blows.

My own view is that slavery may have sharpened the issue in Emerson's mind, but it was not the instigating factor prompting the essay. It was, instead, the issue to be faced naturally after "Compensation" and "Experience" in the sequence of human self-recovery. The rising question in Emerson's mind was, Where in the balance of limitation and freedom can we set the scale? The world seems to give one estimate, the mind another, and our sanity and our spiritual progress are measured where on the scale the needle comes to rest. Here is the crux:

> If we must accept Fate, we are not less compelled to affirm liberty, the significance of the individual, the grandeur of duty, the power of character. This is true, and that other is true. But our geometry cannot span these extreme points, and reconcile them. What to do?

Granted that the arc of this circle is large, perhaps is the topmost curve of the widening spiral of philosophy, just below the concern for Being itself. We understand the limitations of the duration of life, and yet, even here, medical science proposes that down the road, we may solve the problem of aging and that human life might be extended well beyond present limits. Does this mean that even life itself stands within the capacity of human freedom? Or are these matters just relative? After all, life expectancy in some African countries is below forty and in Japan well over eighty. Should we even consider life span as a matter of limitation or destiny except in relation to circumstances?

Emerson's concerns are not with these matters after all. The essay begins with a comment on the Spirit of the Times. He was, then, concerned with events, with slavery, yes, but also with all social issues confronting Americans, and he was speculating on the limits of human action and the solving of intractable problems. But he veered away from the Times rather quickly to address "our own polarity," only to return to politics and society later.

After his grim catalog of nature's deadly disruptions, Emerson begins the process of describing the arc of the geometry involved:

> But these shocks and ruins are less destructive to us, than the stealthy power of other laws which act on us daily. An expense of ends to means is fate; —organization tyrannizing over character. The menagerie, or forms and powers of the spine, is a book of fate: the bill of the bird, the skull of the snake, determines tyrannically its limits. So is the scale of races, of temperaments; so is sex; so is climate; so is the reaction of talents imprisoning the vital power.

In the laws of energy and entropy, we have to see the "expense of ends to means" as inevitable in the workings of nature. This is the first law of fate. The "superfluity of animal, and the defect of thought, in [our] constitution" marks the balance in favor of the animal, hence the emphasis in all religions on sin and behavior. When Emerson says, harshly, "The more of these drones perish, the better for the hive," we have to shudder at his intolerance; and yet, we are reminded again of his declaration in "The Fugitive Slave Law" that he has his own spirits in prison whom no man visits if he does not, which also leaves the rest to themselves.

Those who perish from excess of animal appetite are simply not his concern. It is an example of knowing your work and not being deflected by what is not your concern. Emerson's concern is for those born with a moral bias and those who struggle to extricate themselves from repose.

Once again in "Fate," Emerson finds the theme of reincarnation relevant to the subject:

> It was a poetic attempt to lift this mountain of Fate, to reconcile this despotism of race with liberty, which led the Hindoos to say, "Fate is nothing but the deeds committed in a prior state of existence." I find the coincidence of the extremes of eastern and western speculation in the daring statement of Schelling, "there is in every man a certain feeling, that he has been what he is from all eternity, and by no means became such in time." To say it less sublimely,   in the history of the individual is always an account of his condition, and he knows himself to be a party to his present estate.

Here, Emerson dresses the Hindu figure of fate with a more Western flourish. When the act of reflection takes place in the mind and we actually look at ourselves in the light of thought, we will see that we are indeed a party to our present estate. Our condition in life is a weaving together of nature and nurture *and* election or choice, a fabric of influences colored by innate character. As to nurture, Emerson has always been clear about taking leave of mother and father, of standing aloof of institutions and association and developing self-reliance. He admits the influence of nature and places in opposition to it the inner development of character as balance. Freedom arises from character, less from nature. Insofar as governments grant freedom as an inalienable right, the individual is privileged, but true freedom arises from character and consciousness.

When Emerson used the phrase, "this yet unapproachable America," he was thinking about our awareness as citizens of being a party to the nation's present estate. We have a heritage and no matter how long our ancestors shared it, we find ourselves sharing the fate of a nation as well as our own. I made the point at the outset that few nations in the world share the same "dream," the founders' eloquent sense of promise, or Lincoln's famed Gettysburg Address, which concludes, "that government of the people, by the people, for the people, shall not perish from the earth." These words, now diminished in strength by familiarity, still carry duty and responsibility, as no other nation imposes upon its people. Perhaps some vitality could be returned to Lincoln's words if we added "that government of the people, by enlightened people, for all the people. . . ." It is not merely a dream; it is a fate, a necessity.

> We cannot trifle with this reality, this cropping-out in our planted gardens of the core of the world. No picture of life can have any veracity that does not admit the odious facts. A man's power is hooped in by a necessity, which, by many experiments, he touches on every side, until he learns its arc.

We move through this huge arc of fate and cannot yet see the end or what turn it might make in the direction of freedom or limitation. It is as if Emerson has heard his critics, or anticipates them, and makes certain that the "odious facts" have their day, that it is clear that we are hooped in by necessity.

Those with doubts about that fact need only read the Greek tragic poets to be reminded of the iron bonds of necessity. But what we also learn from the Greeks is that necessity also consorts with justice and heroic rebellion. The Greek *ananke* (necessity) and *dike* (justice) work together in time and space as the gods (laws) see fit, which is to say, not in human time or place. But it is also true that the hero, the extraordinary human, like Antigone, has the freedom to redress the balance in human society in opposition to Destiny.

Although Emerson includes heavy references in the essay to ancient authors, it is his insistence on the everyday, of ordinary life, of *our* fate, that finally engages us. What fate and freedom are to us personally is the focus. If we have done our Emersonian homework, we know the nature and the power of Intellect, how it operates and how it commands the mind.

Intellect annuls Fate. So far as a man thinks, he is free. And though
nothing is more disgusting than the crowing about liberty by slaves,
as most men are, and the flippant mistaking for freedom of some
paper preamble like a "Declaration of Independence," or the statute
right to vote, by those who have never dared to think or to act, yet
it is wholesome to man to look not at Fate, but the other way: the
practical view is the other.

Our more liberal and compassionate sensibilities are initially offended
by Emerson's assault on the sacred images of shackled slaves and the
enshrined Declaration, and yet he is, as usual, correct. We do hear
more whimpering than we see action about our own enslavement in
life's circumstances and more empty saluting at the Declaration without
awareness of what its relevance is to our own destinies. As he said at
the outset, "Our America has a bad name for superficialness." So we
were warned.

What could be a better example of such superficiality than the mind-
less protests about loss of freedom when a new administration tries to
solve pressing national problems? Our friends overseas write and say,
"What on earth is going on over there?" We write back and try to explain
something about the state of knowledge and understanding and the
fear that arises when any genuine change appears imminent. For most
Americans, the word "freedom" means "leave me alone."

As ever, Emerson moves his emphasis to self-culture and the spiritual
conflict between limitation and freedom. "If we rise to spiritual culture,
the antagonism takes a spiritual form." And since the spiritual is always
moral as well, "Fate appears as vindicator, leveling the high, lifting the
low, requiring justice in man, and always striking soon or late, when
justice is not done." If Emerson is correct, a leveling justice will always
prevail in the long run. A pragmatic optimism tells us that justice will
eventually prevail as a matter of fate, or nature, if you will.

This leveling process is also true in our own struggles to move to a higher platform. As we leave behind a morality based on fear and an ethics based on conformity, the old antagonisms will disappear. We will find ourselves acting out of a more universally informed and compassionate sense of justice and moral order. Just as selfish animal instincts are part of our genetic heritage, so too are love and justice; and we imagine these last as evocative of freedom. This tendency for polarity is also part of the system. We act on a daily basis out of antagonisms, and by an effort, we can diffuse that antagonism with insight into its true nature and source.

If we can achieve this insight, to see this way, looking fate in the eye, the overriding power of unity removes the antagonism and we see. It is, indeed a beatitude, a grace, and can carry us across thresholds and through walls. And finally, the insight, so expanding, "as if we grew to worlds" allows us to understand the nature of the consciousness which surrounds us. "It is not in us, but we are in it," Emerson says in this ecstasy of insight. And the remarkable thing is that at this climatic point, we see that the essay has reached only its halfway point.

This remarkable insight culminates, at the close of the essay, in the image of the Beautiful Necessity, again an oxymoron resolving duality.

> Why should we be afraid of Nature, which is no other than "philosophy and theology embodied"? Why should we fear to be crushed by savage elements, we who are made up of the same elements? Let us build to the Beautiful Necessity, which makes man brave in believing that he cannot shun a danger that is appointed, nor incur one that is not; to the Necessity which rudely or softly educates him to the perception that there are no contingencies; that Law rules throughout existence, a Law which is not intelligent but intelligence, —not personal nor impersonal, —it disdains words and passes understanding; it dissolves persons; it vivifies nature; yet solicits the pure in heart to draw on all its omnipotence.

We cannot leave open the question posed by this last assertion, a return to the Law and the question of conscious involvement in the destiny of being human. Are we to accept "a danger that is appointed"? And again, the final assertion is that there are no contingencies, that all actions are lawful and proceed from that lawfulness. But then there is a refinement of sorts. This Law is not intelligent but intelligence, the suggestion that the consciousness that underlies existence is characterized by a transcendent intelligence. The oak outside my window has intelligence in its design from seed to acorn and its defense against the caterpillar. It takes part in an intelligence not altogether its own, as do we.

When the materialist says that the human brain is the most complex organ in the universe, he is declaring the sovereignty of evolution. But if the universe itself possesses an even greater intelligence, to which we have access with our highly developed brains, how great must this immense intelligence be by comparison? After all, the universe has known for billions of years that $E = mc^2$ long before we did the math, and it has been operating on that principle all along. The Beautiful Necessity is the unity we discover when we willingly participate in this intelligence without claiming for ourselves the genius we find.

# 10

# A New Great Awakening

WE IN America are charged with a great deficiency in worship; that reverence does not belong to our character; that our institutions, our polities, and our trade, have fostered a self-reliance which is small, Lilliputians, full of fuss and bustle; we look at and will bear nothing above us in the state, and do exceedingly applaud and admire ourselves, and believe in our senses and understandings, while our imagination and our moral sentiment are desolated. In religion too we want objects above; we are fast losing or have already lost our old reverence; new views of inspiration, of miracles, of the saints, have supplanted the old opinions, and it is vain to bring them again. Revolutions never go backward, and in all churches a certain decay of ancient piety is lamented, and all threatens to lapse into apathy and indifferentism. It becomes us to consider whether we cannot have a real faith and real objects in lieu of these false ones. The human mind, when it is trusted, is never false to itself. If there be sincerity and good meaning—if there be really in us the wish to seek for our superiors, for that which is lawfully above us, we shall not long look in vain.

RWE, "The Sovereignty of Ethics"

Philosophy has developed two main approaches to the fundamental human question of identity, or, Who are we? We can look inward and call the process, as Emerson did, self-recovery, examining the nature of the mind and the human instrument in all its complexity. Or, we can look outward and call it culture. At the present time, it is becoming evident that the latter approach to knowing who we are is the dominant form of exploration, whereas the former remains the method of a smaller group of more esoteric seekers, a community within which you as reader may number yourself.

As a broad examination of current culture reveals, America is experiencing another great awakening, a cultural shift of enormous importance and potential scope. Only a decade ago, such a shift could not have been foreseen. We were then struggling with the dominant influence in politics and social issues of the Religious Right. This political and evangelical movement took power in Washington in 1994 with the Contract for America. Throughout the next six years, conservative evangelicals controlled much of the political agenda and focused attention on what they termed "Family Values."

After the terrorist attacks of September 11, 2001, however, our attention as a culture turned from that narrowly conceived concern with "family values" and began to look outward to the rest of the world. A great new segment of the society, mostly young, woke up to being citizens of the world. The Religious Right turned inward and has since essentially lost its influence and its political power center, while the rest of the country has begun to pay attention to the larger issues of human identity and survival. These concerns center on security, economic recovery, and climate change.

In 2008, the election of Barack Obama confirmed this new sense of larger, global issues. A new vision of America's place and purpose in the world has begun to emerge and define itself. As yet, we are not sure exactly how this new vision will be applied or received, partly because we are also mired in a severe economic crisis which has seized the world's attention. Despite these crises, however, the fact of a crucial awakening holds our national and personal attention.

America has experienced several so-called Great Awakenings. In Emerson's view, the movement of which he was a part began in the 1820s and lasted into the 1840s before being absorbed by the question of slavery. In "Life and Letters in New England" he characterized the religious awakening in a way that describes something of our own transformation:

> It seemed a war between intellect and affection; a crack in nature, which split every church in Christendom into Papal and Protestant; Calvinism into Old and New schools; Quakerism into Old and New; brought new divisions in politics; as the new conscience touching temperance and slavery. The key to the period appeared to be that the mind had become aware of itself. Men grew reflective and intellectual. There was a new consciousness. The former generations acted under the belief that a shining social prosperity was the beatitude of man, and sacrificed uniformly the citizen to the State. The modern mind believed that the nation existed for the individual, for the guardianship and education of every man. This idea, roughly written in revolutions and national movements, in the mind of the philosopher had far more precision; the individual is the world.

The assertion that "the individual is the world" troubles those who would interpret it as saying "I am the most important. I am the world," seeing in it a narrowing of focus, a triumph of the exultant ego over the demands of the broader society. In effect, however, what Emerson did with this assertion was to combine the two modes of philosophical inquiry into a unity. It is the same assertion made in Eastern philosophy when the guru explains that within the human heart is a lotus flower as large as the universe. Inner and outer become the same, and the ego becomes an encumbrance if the individual fails to see clearly.

The new Great Awakening we are experiencing has arisen both

within the human heart and within the dynamics of the American culture. One of the reasons it is taking shape now is not only a reaction to
racial healing and economic crisis, but also to the dramatic change in
our attitude towards external threats. We are now part of the world and
are no longer protected by oceans or border guards. We are living now
in the global village. Security has a different meaning now.

A personal anecdote might illustrate my point. My father entered
the American work force as a chemist and corporate manager in the
1920s. He worked for the same corporation for more than forty years,
rising in the ranks and remaining loyal, just as the company remained
loyal to him. It stayed loyal through the Great Depression, and he, in
turn, never looked at another company, even when he was approached
by competitors. When the company asked him to move to a new city,
he moved. When they asked him to travel, he did, working long hours
without question or complaint. In effect, he was a tenured employee
with a good retirement package.

As I matured through all of this, I could not see any difference
between who my father was and who the company was. They were fused
in my mind as one entity. My father wore the company pin in his lapel
every day of his working life. I'm sure he was not able to separate his
own identity from that of the firm. Its fortunes were his and his theirs.
He fully conformed to corporate identity. He retired in the Sixties.

In the 1980s, all this changed. Corporate loyalty disappeared as companies responded to the pressures of the bottom line. Effective CEOs
were known for being lean and mean. The corporation was no longer
the dependable parent. In turn, workers were no longer loyal either, feeling free now to look elsewhere, which they did in greater and greater
numbers. Mutual suspicion took the place of security and satisfaction in
the workplace. Add to this the decline in the power of organized labor
and the result was rampant insecurity.

This pattern became pervasive among American institutions. One of
the effects was to increase the individual's sense of personal identity once

institutional identity began to dissolve. Emerson knew this phenomenon full well, referring to institutions as associations. In "Heroism," an essay devoted to individual self-recovery, he advised, "I see not any road of perfect peace which a man can walk, but after the counsel of his own bosom. Let him quit too much association, let him go home much, and stablish himself in those courses he approves."

The principle holds for all time not spent in solitude. Emerson's plea is to withhold ourselves from association in order to find the way in which the larger Self incarnates itself in us. In *Essays I* he makes a series of strong assertions, compounding the broader theme of this volume of essays—which builds from "History" and moves through "Self-Reliance" and then the spiritual essays, to conclude with "Intellect" and "Art." In "Friendship," a central essay in that volume, he observed, "Almost all people descend to meet. All association must be a compromise, and, what is worst, the very flower and aroma of the flower of each of the beautiful natures disappears as they approach each other." And when institutions are involved, the pressure is even greater. Consider, for instance, the "aroma of the flower" as the lotus within the heart.

A strong symbol of what is happening today is the weakening of the authority of Christian Fundamentalism in America, not just in the light of radical fundamentalism abroad, but also in a new wariness of the dubious voice of authority, not to mention the weakness of those in positions of authority as scandal after scandal breaks over them. When we compare Emerson's voice to that of Fundamentalist authority, we begin to see why and how things are changing. Such a comparison reveals a certain stance in relation to the need for obedience of authority.

It is axiomatic that when security fails and we are left to our own devises, we do one of two things: develop self-reliance or seek out a comforting association. In his 2007 book *The Conservative Soul,* Andrew Sullivan describes the crucial moment in the life of a religious fundamentalist when he or she surrenders personal autonomy in order to merge with the chosen doctrine:

For the fundamentalist, there is one moment of real conscience, the moment when he makes the decision to conform his mind and will to an external authority. After that, his sole task is obedience, or, at best, being the best student in a class where there is only one set of right answers, prescribed beforehand (and you're allowed, in fact compelled, to see the answers in advance).

The key here is the image of knowing the answers in advance, as opposed, for example, to spiritual work under the guidance of a teacher who does not provide answers in advance and who, although demanding obedience and standing as authority, does so from a wholly different source than we see in fundamentalist contexts. For the fundamentalist this moment "of real conscience" seeks to obliterate the past in favor of a new life in obedience to a new authority. The principle reduced to a bumper sticker is "Let go, let God."

In Emerson's idealism, the similar moment of conscience reflects the personal commitment to self-trust in which all authority moves within and the conscience itself fully awakens; but in the case of Idealism, the previous life is not rejected. Rather, it is reflected upon and integrated into a new perception.

In the case of the fundamentalist, the external authority to which all obedience is due has to hammer away at the conscience with its doctrinal principles and teaching, molding its message to the new reality if the person is to be "saved." If the conscience shows any reluctance or doubt, the teaching intensifies until all doubt is wiped clean or the individual either submits or rebels and rejects the authority.

In the case of idealism, the challenge comes when the individual faces for the first time the complexities of obedience to a newly perceived inner authority. If external authority is not to be trusted, can internal resources be trusted? How can the individual separate from the cacophony that is the ordinary mind to find the wise silence within? Emerson's task, once he made the choice to trust the authority of his own mind, was to address the nature and actions of self-trust.

In "Self-Reliance" he went straight at the problem.

Nothing is at last sacred but the integrity of your own mind. Absolve you to yourself, and you shall have the suffrage of the world. I remember an answer which when quite young I was prompted to make to a valued adviser, who was wont to importune me with the dear old doctrines of the church. On my saying, What have I to do with the sacredness of traditions, if I live wholly from within? my friend suggested, — "But these impulses may be from below, not from above." I replied, "They do not seem to me to be such; but if I am the Devil's child, I will live then from the Devil." No law can be sacred to me but that of my nature.

Imagine for a moment the fundamentalist reading this passage, with its seemingly cavalier reference to being the Devil's child. What Emerson knew, of course, was that the real test of who or what is in control of our lives is measured by the character of the lives we actually lead. The last line of that passage is the crux. If "no law can be sacred to me but that of my nature," the test is to determine what that nature consists in; and here the debate rages on, mostly these days among biologists. When Jesus was asked the same question he used the analogy of the fruit tree, saying that a sound tree will bring forth life-giving fruit. The crucial line in Matthew 7 is, "Wherefore by their fruits ye shall know them." Our actions are the measure.

Do our genes dictate a violent streak in our nature? Are we fundamentally driven by our DNA to behave in predetermined patterns, or worse, are we susceptible to "evil" forces "out there" to commit terrible acts? Or, in another albeit fading sphere, does the Freudian unconscious hold sway? Does it control our behavior in ways we fail to comprehend? Are we deluded into thinking we have free will? Answers to these important questions will arise in the reflective mind seeking to know itself and willing to remain in the present moment.

For the rest of his creative life, Emerson addressed the question of "my nature" in a variety of ways and under the subject headings of individual and collective culture. He was taken to task any number of times for minimizing the presence of evil in the world and in human nature. His central view was that evil is merely privation, the absence of good, of conscience, and not a force or entity opposing good or God. Emerson certainly acknowledged the full range of nature's grotesque and savage character and the human part in it. He was not naive. This fullness, range, and mystery in human nature is what marks Emerson worthy of our attention. This range comes to our attention most clearly in the essays contained in *Conduct of Life*.

In 1860, Emerson published a series of essays that he had been using as lectures for a decade. *Conduct of Life* was his contribution to addressing the ordinary, that is, the daily life of people in a time of war. In the essay "Worship," he offered some balance to his essays on Fate, Power, and Wealth, having heard the complaint that he might be offering too much acknowledgment to the "evil spirit of the times."

If "Worship" was meant to be palliative, it certainly did not begin in a soothing tone. Emerson addressed the fundamentalist tendencies of the time in no uncertain terms.

> A silent revolution has loosed the tension of the old religious sects, and, in place of the gravity and permanence of those societies of opinion, they run into freak and extravagance. In creeds never was such levity; witness the heathenisms in Christianity, the periodic "revivals," the Millennium mathematics, the peacock ritualism, the retrogression to Popery, the maundering of Mormons, the squalor of Mesmerism, the deliration of rappings, the rat and mouse revelation, thumps in table-drawers, and black art. The architecture, the music, the prayer, partake of the madness: the arts sink into shift and make-believe.

Faced with this circus, what is the truth-seeking human being to do? He or she might just vow, as Emerson did in his Divinity School Address, "to church no more." Not even fellowship and common social values could overcome the polarities of good and evil and the loss of "the mystic offices of Christ," as he phrased it in "Worship."

What is the destiny of a country devoted to the dualism of good and evil, to see operating in every disaster the influence of some consciously malevolent force? Our former president saw evil operating in the world, not just evil as immoral action, but, as he said, evil as entity. We were engaged, he claimed, in a battle with pure evil, a Satanic force unleashed in the world by forces opposing truth, justice, and freedom. George W. Bush said that the terrorists out there hate us because we are free. They hate freedom, he declared. This was the voice of a deluded fundamentalism. Fortunately, it appears that this kind of radical dualism is being set aside in favor of a new approach to defeating those bent on violence and terrorism. Perhaps in the future we will give our attention to violent individuals and groups and not to abstract malevolent forces.

In the second half of "Fate," Emerson looks at the effects of seeing the world in these radical polarities when we try to change our perceptions:

> Now whether, seeing these two things, fate and power, we are permitted to believe in unity? The bulk of mankind believe in two gods. They are under one dominion here in the house, as friend and parent, in social circles, in letters, in art, in love, in religion: but in mechanics, in dealing with steam and climate, in trade, in politics, they think they come under another; and that it would be a practical blunder to transfer the method and way of working of one sphere, into the other. What good, honest, generous men at home, will be wolves and foxes on change! What pious men in the parlor will vote for what reprobates at the polls! To a certain point, they believe themselves in the care of a Providence. But, in a steamboat, in an epidemic, in war, they believe a malignant energy rules.

A malignant energy? Is there a universal force in the actions of human beings other than the result of individual human defect or ignorance? At the level of law in the universe, can there be the kind of spiritual opposition that creates and sustains destructive and malevolent ends? Can the madness now prevalent in the world—the crises of hunger, disease, and violence—be cosmic? Or is it, as Emerson thought, the result of privation, a function of ignorance, greed, and bigotry?

In nature, of course, we are quick to describe what appears to be cruelty and murders left and right as malignant as opposed to the natural facts of hunger and survival. Do we really think that the lion will lie down with the lamb? Isn't the lamb a fit meal for hungry cubs back in the den? It was Ortega who said that the tiger could not be "de-tiger-ized" but a human being could be dehumanized. It is a salient point. If we are, indeed, homo sapiens, knowing man, is it not possible to end cruelty and ignorance by intelligent melioration? What else can "knowing" mean?

In other ways, the study of theology is also devoted to the nature of God; and within that study is the question of the forces characteristic of gods. Was Emerson perhaps blinded by his determination to see Platonic Good as the only driving force in the cosmos? Is he irrelevant as a serious thinker because he does not see evil as a reality in the world? Is he, as one detractor said, simply too cheery?

Emerson insists in "Fate" that rather than a malevolent force, evil can be described as "unpenetrated causes." It is force not comprehended by the understanding but still circumscribed by the laws of nature. If America, for example, sees itself opposed in the world by forces of evil, then we, logically, must be the representatives of Good. It would not be possible in this way of thinking that anything we do could be evil or driven by the forces of evil. If that were the case, then the terrorists must be followers of the Good. This absurd reasoning is a direct result of misunderstanding the nature of fate and its interplay with power.

Similarly, our adversaries in this "war on terror" —the insurgents, the terrorists, the Islamic warriors, whatever label we choose to use—are also engulfed in this destructive dualistic imagery, fighting for the "Good" as they see it, against the Satanic Empire that is America. Recently, in a film of a Baghdad bombing, an insurgent was seen running off and turning to shout, "God is great!" Being trapped in this warped religious ideology, neither party can approach the other as an entity to be bargained with in good faith. There can be no sane dialogue in a confrontation between good and evil. Does God bargain with Satan? Can Satan apologize and give up his apostasy? In a literal sense, the questions are absurd.

Another argument, the usual one, is that all conflict between limitation and ideas of freedom is merely human prejudices and power struggles taking place in an indifferent universe. We perceive that we live in a predicament and must find our way out as best we can. If opposed, we retaliate in kind. If thwarted, we either retreat or find another way forward. In other words, there are no "forces" in this view, just resistance like friction, part of Newton's universe of fundamental laws. Life is finding a way to get what we need and want, resistance assumed. All differences in limitation and freedom are accidents of birth and circumstances.

Does this sound depressing? Emerson thought so. It presupposes a meaningless universe with no teleological framework, in which we must conjure our own meaning and rationalize our actions as best we can. The difficulty with this vision is that such meanings are hollow at the core, and we know it. It is that very hollowness that invokes the religious instinct and creates the doctrines which support it. Emerson's philosophy wants more than conjuring and more than arbitrary illusions to fill up empty spaces. Emerson represents the life-enhancing middle ground.

Emerson's answer to this hollow view in "Fate" is found in a conscious nature. "Nature is intricate, overlapped, interweaved, and endless." Emerson uses an example of Christopher Wren saying of the beautiful King's College chapel that if anybody would tell him where to lay the first stone, he would build such another. Emerson then carries the analogy further by asking, "But where shall we find the first atom in this house of man, which is all consent, inosculation, and balance of parts?" Note that in the example Emerson finds to support the first assertion is a human artifact rather than a natural one, implying as it does the human fully in tune with nature and building upon it. We don't use words like "inosculation" anymore, but in its meaning of "intimately connected" it reflects perfectly the sense that Wren intended in his relation of the chapel to nature. The chapel and nature were intertwined like fibers in a plant, naturally gathered to make a unified organic statement.

So too with all human endeavor when we are in harmony with the laws of nature, as opposed to a structure that stands separate from its surroundings, white and stark against the landscape so as to make a statement of dominance, like a Puritan church in a town square designed to stake out sacred territory aversive to nature, which, in turn, was perceived to be hostile and even demonic. This notion of church as sanctuary creates separation and also creates nature as a place from which we seek refuge and avoid danger.

Emerson was a radical thinker, as all great thinkers are. As he said, watch out when a thinker is let loose in the world. We may be seeing signs of it now, even in the midst of this combustible age in which all barriers of taste and restraint have been dropped from debate and conversation. Emerson's radical mind never expressed itself in offensive language, but rather in radical assertions of the truth as he perceived it. As we have seen, his subjects ranged through the varieties of ordinary life: household, commerce, society, and religion in particular, and all felt the sting of his barbs, and although he did devote a book to the English, his concern and true subject was America, this yet unapproachable America.

The radical Emerson emerges most clearly in the convergence of American culture with its religious practices. He saw clearly what happens when religions stagnate and fail to respond to crying need. Wringing our hands in despair, we pray that God will solve the problem. Here is Emerson in "Worship."

> Not knowing what to do, we ape our ancestors; the churches stagger backward to the mummeries of the dark ages. By the irresistible maturing of the general mind, the Christian traditions have lost their hold. The dogma of the mystic offices of Christ being dropped, and he standing on his genius as a moral teacher, 'tis impossible to maintain the old emphasis of his personality; and it recedes, as all persons

must, before the sublimity of the moral laws. From this change, and in the momentary absence of any religious genius that could offset the immense material activity, there is a feeling that religion is gone.

If gone, or going, what takes its place? For Emerson, reality consists of the conscious individual in the world. If we are awake, we operate most of the time as individuals within the contexts of social structures—the churches, colleges, governments, and companies within which inevitably we find ourselves—seeking there to develop what powers of our own we can nurture along with others of like mind, in the name of moral and ethical action.

Are there dangers in this vision? Of course. In his recent book *American Transcendentalism,* Philip Gura points out the dangers of Emerson's call to spiritual self-reliance. Elizabeth Peabody, one of the most astute and able among Emerson's Concord circle, saw the danger in his radical message and referred to it as ego-theism, the erroneous inflation of the ego as a result of a mistaken spiritual exultation. It is the same error of interpretation that erroneously links Emerson with Ayn Rand's ego-theism. The Greeks knew a great deal about spiritual exultation and called it hubris. We see it in those who tell us they speak to and for God and who tell us what God wants for and from us. Another example from Gura's account is the observation from Henry James, Sr., when he said, "The curse of our present times . . . [is] the selfhood imposed on us by an evil world."

As Gura argues, Emerson's insistence on withdrawal, as manifested clearly enough in "The Transcendentalist," is an indictment of the movement, not its virtue, even though, in the 1850s, Emerson took to the lectern (if not the streets) to join the Abolitionists. I would argue that Emerson knew full well that in order to act morally in the world, the individual needs first to develop a powerful and secure self-trust, and this self-trust requires a period of incubation before its emergence in the world. It is an argument without a resolution, however, since we can never know what is taking place within the individual human soul prior to finding its place in the world, where action is the measure and words its clarion call.

What seems clear, however, is that at the present time we are experiencing a shift in American life—both among individuals and institutions, and perhaps in its politics—in the direction of effective action against the crying needs of our time: poverty, disease, hunger, and environmental degradation. Whether or not this shift is the result of an enlightened individualism or becomes the role of an activist government remains an open question.

# 11
# Wealth and Economy

THE gloomy catastrophe of a bankruptcy, of a revolution, of a war, which wrap cities and nations in black, is only an emphatic exposition of the natural results of given courses of action, as we look at a pod to learn the virtues of a plant.

RWE, Journal, November 1837

The crisis that now faces America and many of the world's advanced and emerging economies will not end by restoring what has been. Something very new is being born, and no one person or party knows what the form of that something will be. Regardless of when and how some economic order is established, what is most certain is that fundamental change is taking place in how individuals and nations will flourish or fail.

Emerson's essay "Wealth" speaks to change, transformation, and principle in matters of how we make our way in the world. The essay begins with a principle: "Every man is a consumer, and ought to be a producer. He fails to make his place good in the world, unless he not only pays his debt, but also adds something to the common wealth."

Whatever takes place in the coming transformation, this one principle will have to be obeyed.

It is a given that people normally consume food, energy, natural resources, and manufactured goods of all kinds. We pay for what we consume and as a result sometimes incur debt, which we are obliged to pay through what we produce through work. Emerson put the matter plainly in "Compensation" when he said, "You must pay at last your own debt." If he had said, merely, "You must pay your debts," the point would have been made too weakly. "At last" makes the point that we cannot avoid paying the debts we owe. Even in death, debt lingers and must be paid by those who remain. The word "own" hammers the point home.

It may appear, in reading "Wealth" that the subject matter is outdated with its references to steam, coal, and lamp wicks, but any attentive reader easily transfers the terms to today's oil and power grids. No matter the age, nature is still the stern mistress. When times are hard for the individual who is without means or easy work, wants become hard. Emerson says, "[Nature] starves, taunts, and torments him, takes away warmth, laughter, sleep, friends, and daylight, until he has fought his way to his own loaf. Then, less peremptorily, but still with sting enough, she urges him to the acquisition of such things as belong to him."

Emerson's theme in the essay is wealth, not bare survival. We are meant to be rich, he claims, against the advice of the philosophers who argue "the greatness of man [is] in making his wants few." Can this be right? Surely we can't all be rich, at least as a result of Nature's design. Emerson himself, however, was a prime example of the principle he urges. By the end of the Civil War, when his daughter married into the Forbes family of Boston, Emerson's financial position, with the help of his new son-in-law, improved until he was listed as one of the ten wealthiest men in Massachusetts. But poverty was his estate for the first half of life. He knew the struggle. But material wealth was not his only theme.

Rich is a relative term. We are rich when we have a tight roof over our heads, oil in the tank, a working car in the driveway, food on the table, savings in the bank, and most important, manageable debt, or, better yet, no debt at all. According to the Federal Reserve, the average American household in 2008 carried nearly $8,700 in credit card debt. The Reserve also claims, however, that more than half of American households (56 percent) carry little or no debt at all, a fact which testifies to the tyranny of averages. Certainly some debt is inevitable—emergency health care, college tuition, and temporary joblessness. But most of it is from voluntarily spending more than we earn as a matter of perceived need, habit, or desire. Much of that debt also relates to fear of what we imagine poverty to be. Before riches there lies poverty for many of us, and in the latter state exist both physical and moral struggle.

> The subject of economy mixes itself with morals, inasmuch as it is a peremptory point of virtue that a man's independence be secured. Poverty demoralizes. A man in debt is so far a slave; and Wall-street thinks it easy for a millionaire to be a man of his word, a man of honor, but, that, in failing circumstances, no man can be relied on to keep his integrity.

"Wealth" describes our own times with such devastating accuracy that we know there are universal principles at work, not unique circumstances. Still, though, is this claim of Emerson's that we ought to be rich not a gross failure of judgment, given the billions in the world who seem without the faintest possibility of even a modest improvement in their circumstances? Emerson was certainly aware himself of poverty throughout the world in which he traveled. The word "rich" then had a different meaning.

> Is not then the demand to be rich legitimate? Yet, I have never seen a rich man. I have never seen a man as rich as all men ought to be, or, with an adequate command of nature. The pulpit and the press have many commonplaces denouncing the thirst for wealth; but if men should take these moralists at their word, and leave off aiming to be

rich, the moralists would rush to rekindle at all hazards this love of power in the people, lest civilization should be undone. . . . Man was born to be rich, or, inevitably grows rich by the use of his faculties; by the union of thought with nature. Property is an intellectual production. The game requires coolness, right reasoning, promptness, and patience in the players. Cultivated labor drives out brute labor. An infinite number of shrewd men, in infinite years, have arrived at certain best and shortest ways of doing, and this accumulated skill in arts, cultures, harvestings, curings, manufactures, navigations, exchanges, constitutes the worth of our world to-day.

As institutions and governments on every level struggle to manage the wild swings of the economy, we find ourselves debating the merits of active engagement or benign neglect, trying to find the right formula to bring our affairs into some kind of just balance. We admire and respect the principles of the free market and yet fear its cycles and decry its unregulated abuses. Emerson, too, engaged in this debate and offered in "Wealth" this observation:

Wealth brings with it its own checks and balances. The basis of political economy is non-interference. The only safe rule is found in the self-adjusting meter of demand and supply. Do not legislate. Meddle, and you snap the sinews with your sumptuary laws. Give no bounties: make equal laws: secure life and property, and you need not give alms. Open the doors of opportunity to talent and virtue, and they will do themselves justice, and property will not be in bad hands. In a free and just commonwealth, property rushes from the idle and imbecile, to the industrious, brave, and persevering.

On one hand here he appears to be the conservative demanding non-interference, minimizing the "sumptuary" laws of undue regulation. On the other, however, as the progressive he demands the creation of laws guaranteeing that every individual, rich or poor, has the opportunity to test his or her skills in a "free and just commonwealth." In such a state, those without the character to take advantage of those just and equal laws will give way to those who possess "the right stuff." It is not clear how the present administration will find the right balance of regulation and progressive laws to meet Emerson's "safe rule."

If Emerson had encountered the complexities and abuses of the present capital markets, he would, I believe, have rested on principle and minimal rules. He knew that the only "safe rule" was the nature's own law of supply and demand. In the human world, the principle of equal protection under the law had to be upheld. In our own crisis, we may find that the imposition of stiff regulation will ultimately harm the operation of political economy and that the only effective controls will be those that nature imposes. He would, however, watch carefully for those who would manipulate the natural system unlawfully. As we learned in the present crisis, the watchdogs were asleep while the foxes ravaged the hen-house.

"Wealth" is the practical application of Emerson's earlier "Compensation," the essay that sets out the laws of nature. These laws expressed themselves in the sayings of the day:

> All things are double, one against another. — Tit for tat; an eye for an eye; a tooth for a tooth; blood for blood; measure for measure; love for love. — Give and it shall be given you. — He that watereth shall be watered himself. — What will you have? quoth God; pay for it and take it. — Nothing venture, nothing have. — Thou shalt be paid exactly for what thou hast done, no more, no less. — Who doth not work shall not eat. — Harm watch, harm catch. — Curses always recoil on the head of him who imprecates them. — If you put a chain around the neck of a slave, the other end fastens itself around your own. — Bad counsel confounds the adviser.

All governments and legislators need to have these sayings, or ones brought up to date, hung on their walls, and the central one of them all—What will you have, quoth God; pay for it and take it—in bold. It's the "pay for it" that we neglect. As a nation, we are unwilling (or unable) to face the debt we owe ourselves. In such an environment, I for one am even more determined to leave my children something when I die, not as a legacy but as a partial payment for the debt we as a country are going to leave to them to pay. I only hope they don't have to add to it before their turn comes.

Ask Americans now what concerns them most, they say "the economy." Emerson's lecture with that title did not make it into *The Conduct of Life* series and so it remains unread except by specialists. It appears now in *The Later Lectures*, published by the University of Georgia Press in 2001. The two lectures delivered together were nonetheless very popular with audiences, being as they were practical and presenting examples common to their experience.

The key to "Economy" is the application of principle to natural law. Nature is the first economist, Emerson tells us, and then he branches out to draw the inferences and explain. This essay, composed late in his career, has echoes to earlier work, namely, including *Nature,* "Compensation," and "The Over-Soul." Here in "Economy" Emerson recapitulates a major theme in his universal vision of humanity's place in nature.

> I said, the other evening, that, Nature peremptorily requires that each must feed himself. She sends each man into the world armed with some faculty which enables him with ease and pleasure to do something which no other can do, and so to make himself necessary to society. I have to say this very often but Nature says it oftener than I. It is a clownish merit to insist on doing all things with one's own hands, as if every man should build a clumsy house, forge his hammer and nails, knead and bake his dough; another can do it better and cheaper; but it is his essential virtue, to dare to do what he believes and loves, if his skill lie in taming horses, or in laying out gardens, or in sailing a ship, or in writing musical scores, let him leave all and do that.

It is the idealist reference to "ease and pleasure" that makes these passages stand out and demand to be clarified. He had the experience of written eloquence, performed, to be sure, in short segments as essays, but nonetheless with relative ease. He had a gift, and recognizing it soon enough, he designed a life around its potential to feed himself and his family. And certainly, eloquence is one of the talents we can nourish and then put to practical use. It also comes under the category of production.

In an even more idealistic passage in "The Over-Soul," he let out the reins of his eloquence on the subject of talent and ease in work. Speaking about our habit of agonizing over the choices of occupation and mode of living, he is reassuring, while at the same time pointed in his admonitions. The relevant passage appears in full as Appendix I on page 151.

Behaving irresponsibly is a function of living without adult duties or responsibilities, where life is managed for us from womb to tomb without the challenges that nature demands of all creatures. At present, America is going through the trials of finding a healthy balance between leaving the individual free to succeed or fail alone and the welfare state where risk and error are minimized or virtually eliminated. The Obama administration is not bent on the latter, that is clear from Obama's own writings, but conservatives and libertarians try to paint him into that corner, using such words as "socialism" and "welfare state" to prevent the passage of a more just and rational health care system and greater opportunity for good jobs and higher education for all who seek it.

Emerson's principles of non-interference and equal laws are the balanced means to a just end. These principles applied to the individual also apply to larger spheres, to the family, community, state, nation, and world. The word "economy" in micro-economics means thrift and good management and only later means the prosperity and earnings of a certain place. Emerson's genius saw clearly the unity of these principles applied to ordinary and higher life. If we are not fragmented in our lives between thought and action, between our inner and outward lives, we are in a state or place where inner and outer economy are one. Toward the end of "Wealth" Emerson sums up and connects the role of the capitalist to the laws of nature.

The counting-room maxims liberally expounded are laws of the Universe. The merchant's economy is a coarse symbol of the soul's economy. It is, to spend for power, and not for pleasure. It is to invest income; that is to say, to take up particulars into generals; days into integral eras, —literary, emotive, practical, of its life, and still to ascend in its investment. The merchant has but one rule, absorb and invest: he is to be capitalist: the scraps and filings must be gathered back into the crucible; the gas and smoke must be burned, and earnings must not go to increase expense, but to capital again. Well, the man must be capitalist. Will he spend his income, or will he invest? His body and every organ is under the same law. His body is a jar, in which the liquor of life is stored. Will he spend for pleasure? The way to ruin is short and facile. Will he not spend, but hoard for power? It passes through the sacred fermentations, by that law of Nature whereby everything climbs to higher platforms, and bodily vigor becomes mental and moral vigor.

For some, the word "capitalist" will never be an attractive or positive title, especially in our own time when greed and financial criminality lie exposed. Emerson's use of the term, however, is meant to apply to any individual who makes his or her way in the world by investing time, energy, attention, skill, determination, and courage using the talents we have been given. Talent is the capital we invest. The key, as always for Emerson, is the unity of minute and cosmic laws and our responsibility to follow those laws in our own economic pursuits.

# 12
# America as Opportunity

THIS book began with a quotation from "American Civilization."
I would like to repeat some of it here as we reach the conclusion of this enterprise.

> Why cannot the best civilization be extended over the whole country,
> since the disorder of the less-civilized portion menaces the existence of
> the country? Is this secular progress we have described, this evolution
> of man to the highest powers, only to give him sensibility, and not
> to bring duties with it? Is he not to make his knowledge practical? to
> stand and to withstand? Is not civilization heroic also? Is it not for
> action? has it not a will?

The Emerson of 1862, when the Civil War raged with no end in
sight and with the question of winner and loser uncertain, was focused
on the immediate question of freeing the slaves. Emerson argued that
the Emancipation Proclamation, sitting unsigned in President Lincoln's
desk, should be put into effect immediately, as a matter of both principle
and practicality. And as it happened the Union victory at Antietam that
fall provided Lincoln the opportunity to issue the Proclamation. That
decision changed the nature of the war.

If we look at Emerson's address today, his words speak to us again. Indeed, why cannot the best civilization be extended over the whole country? Does our moral sensibility give us only some vague sense of purpose but not carry with it the will and means to practical applications? As I write this, President Obama is fighting to pass health care legislation, attempting to raise the level of American civilization to that higher level where all Americans can be covered and we can join other civilized countries in providing that basic right.

Emerson proclaimed the fundamental value of the Dream of America when he said, "We live in a new and exceptional age. America is another word for Opportunity." It is the time for this new generation in this new century to demonstrate how America will define opportunity. What is striking is that the words slavery and emancipation both carry over from America's defining conflict to this time.

Deeper into his lecture Emerson drove the point home, urging those in power to rise above argument and to make a commitment to principle.

> In this national crisis, it is not argument that we want, but that rare courage which dares commit itself to a principle, believing that Nature is its ally, and will create the instruments it requires, and more than make good any petty and injurious profit which it may disturb. There never was such a combination as this of ours, and the rules to meet it are not set down in any history. We want men of original perception and original action, who can open their eyes wider than to a nationality, namely, to considerations of benefit to the human race, can act in the interest of civilization.

The same advice can be applied to our current leaders. The petty concerns of party and election prospects pale before the necessity to make the changes required, not just to solve the health care crisis but also to address the other critical problems facing the country: energy, environment, education, and war. As if these problems were not enough to face and solve, we also have to look both home and abroad to address the ancient problems of slavery and emancipation.

UNICEF estimates that 200,000 children from West and Central Africa are sold into slavery each year, and that over 20 million people today are held as slaves throughout the world. And by slavery we don't mean just low-paying jobs, but actual slaves held forcibly in bondage. Emancipation means not only taking action to free such individuals, but also to liberate the millions of women held in virtual slavery through the power of fundamentalist religion supported by national policy.

On a slightly lesser scale, here in America there are millions of workers earning less than a decent living wage, indebted and forced to keep quiet for fear of violence or homelessness for themselves and their children. It is debt bondage, slaves to circumstance with no clear relief in sight. As Emerson urged, we want leaders who can open their eyes and can act in the interest of civilization. The secret then and now is a true emancipation—freedom from bondage of every kind.

> The one power that has legs long enough and strong enough to wade across the Potomac offers itself at this hour; the one strong enough to bring all the civility up to the height of that which is best, prays now at the door of Congress for leave to move. Emancipation is the demand of civilization. That is a principle; everything else is an intrigue. This is a progressive policy, puts the whole people in healthy, productive, amiable position, puts every man in the South in just and natural relations with every man in the North, laborer with laborer.

The same Potomac that flowed then flows now, and again we wait for Congress to move. The move, however, has to be enlightened and responsible at the same time. We cannot act out of panic as we did after the disaster of 9/11 when Congress passed a war resolution without sufficient knowledge and with too much trust in a deceptive administration.

It is the hallmark of a civilized nation when it encourages and helps its people secure the basic necessities of life, and the three most important are these: the opportunity to work and earn a living wage, the right

to a safe and secure place to live, and a health care system responsive
to basic needs.

Emerson addressed the relationship between a civilized society and
a safe and secure place to live in this following passage from "Civilization." The first of these is work.

> The division of labor, the multiplication of the arts of peace, which
> is nothing but a large allowance to each man to choose his work
> according to his faculty, —to live by his better hand, —fills the State
> with useful and happy laborers; and they, creating demand by the very
> temptation of their productions, are rapidly and surely rewarded by
> good sale: and what a police and ten commandments their work thus
> becomes. So true is Dr. Johnson's remark that "men are seldom more
> innocently employed than when they are making money."

American civilization forgot this basic principle when the Reagan
administration sought to control inflation by effectively freezing ordinary
wages with its devotion to "trickle down economics." Cutting taxes for
the rich was meant to put more money into the hands of those who
could best invest it and "raise all boats," or so went the argument. But
the reverse happened. Money began to gather at the top to effectively
rob those lower on the economic scale. The result was that the credit
card became the increase in wages required to sustain the necessities of
life. The principle of opportunity was forgotten. The second principle of
the enlightened civilization is housing, again addressed by Emerson:

> Where shall we begin or end the list of those feats of liberty and
> wit, each of which feats made an epoch of history? Thus the effect
> of a framed or stone house is immense on the tranquillity, power and
> refinement of the builder. A man in a cave or in a camp, a nomad,
> will die with no more estate than the wolf or the horse leaves. But so
> simple a labor as a house being achieved, his chief enemies are kept
> at bay. He is safe from the teeth of wild animals, from frost, sun-
> stroke and weather; and fine faculties begin to yield their fine harvest.
> Invention and art are born, manners and social beauty and delight.

'T is wonderful how soon a piano gets into a log hut on the frontier. You would think they found it under a pine stump. With it comes a Latin grammar, —and one of those tow-head boys has written a hymn on Sunday. Now let colleges, now let senates take heed! for here is one who opening these fine tastes on the basis of the pioneer's iron constitution, will gather all their laurels in his strong hands.

Various attempts have been made to make safe and secure housing available to all Americans. The current economic crisis was created by good intentions at the top of government that were subverted by greed and ignorance at the bottom of society. Once corrected by cooler heads and a heavy dose of education and self-reliance, we may find our way back to Emerson's sense of "tranquillity, power and refinement." It is not an idle dream. Progressives have argued for years that adequate housing for middle and low income earners is the sign of a sound culture as well as a sound economy. And yet we still have the homeless, and the poor living in substandard housing, throughout the wealthiest country in the world.

The final point, the matter of health and general well-being, is a much larger issue than reform of the health care system. Health must be physical, psychological, and spiritual. Emerson speaks eloquently of all three areas, as we see from previous chapters. In another essay from the same period, "Considerations by the Way," he had this to say about health:

If now in this connection of discourse, we should venture on laying down the first obvious rules of life, I will not here repeat the first rule of economy, already propounded once and again, that every man shall maintain himself, —but I will say, get health. No labor, pains, temperance, poverty, nor exercise, that can gain it, must be grudged. For sickness is a cannibal which eats up all the life and youth it can lay hold of, and absorbs its own sons and daughters. I figure it as a pale, wailing, distracted phantom, absolutely selfish, heedless of what is good and great, attentive to its sensations, losing its soul, and afflict-

ing other souls with meanness and mopings, and with ministration
to its voracity of trifles.

We all know, who have lived long enough, the truth of this statement.
Sickness is indeed a cannibal eating up life and youth, and of course
eating up the resources of the country as well. We can only estimate
how many Americans suffer and wither away in body and mind in the
absence of fundamental health care. Those who oppose universal care
for the American people have failed a major moral test. It is a matter of
being civilized. And what exactly is civilization? How is it defined?

I add this last observation by Emerson, what for him defines civilization. Emerson makes the clear connection here between the role of
women in society and the degree to which that society is civilized.

> Right position of woman in the State is another index. Poverty and
> industry with a healthy mind read very easily the laws of humanity, and
> love them: place the sexes in right relations of mutual respect, and a
> severe morality gives that essential charm to woman which educates all
> that is delicate, poetic and self-sacrificing; breeds courtesy and learn-
> ing, conversation and wit, in her rough mate; so that I have thought
> a sufficient measure of civilization is the influence of good women.

In the years between 1850, when the Fugitive Slave Law roused
him to become an activist to end slavery, until 1862 when he traveled
to Washington to plead for passage of the Emancipation Proclamation,
Ralph Waldo Emerson emerged from his study onto the public stage.
His emergence signaled the birth of idealism as an instrument of political action. This emergence was not Emerson's alone, of course, but as
a major public figure, his commitment meant that the Civil War was
now about a moral principle and not just about commercial interests
and national unity. The conflict became a struggle for human dignity
and individual freedom.

In our own time, the election of Barack Obama has signaled a rebirth
of idealism, having similar energy and purpose. No longer do conserva-

tives hold the high moral ground, having lost it through the hypocrisies and failures of the last Bush administration. To be sure, economic and "pocketbook" issues will still influence elections, but the tone has changed in America. Given economic recovery, albeit with significant changes in how such a recovery will look, the country is posed to address those principled needs we have been describing here.

As we approach 2012 and beyond, we may see a realization of the ideals Emerson articulated for what he called "this yet unapproachable America."

# Appendix I –
# Passage from "Spiritual Laws"

A LITTLE consideration of what takes place around us every day would show us, that a higher law than that of our will regulates events; that our painful labors are unnecessary, and fruitless; that only in our easy, simple, spontaneous action are we strong, and by contenting ourselves with obedience we become divine. Belief and love, —a believing love will relieve us of a vast load of care. O my brothers, God exists. There is a soul at the centre of nature, and over the will of every man, so that none of us can wrong the universe. It has so infused its strong enchantment into nature, that we prosper when we accept its advice, and when we struggle to wound its creatures, our hands are glued to our sides, or they beat our own breasts. The whole course of things goes to teach us faith. We need only obey. There is guidance for each of us, and by lowly listening we shall hear the right word. Why need you choose so painfully your place, and occupation, and associates, and modes of action, and of entertainment? Certainly there is a possible right for you that precludes the need of balance and wilful election. For you there is a reality, a fit place and congenial duties. Place yourself in the middle of the stream of power and wisdom which animates all whom it floats, and you are without effort impelled to truth, to right, and a perfect contentment. Then you put all gainsayers in the wrong. Then you are the world, the measure of right, of truth, of beauty. If we will not be mar-plots with our miserable interferences, the work, the society, letters, arts, science, religion of men would go on far better than now, and the heaven predicted from the beginning of the world, and still predicted from the bottom of the heart, would organize itself, as do now the rose, and the air, and the sun.

I say, *do not choose;* but that is a figure of speech by which I would distinguish what is commonly called *choice* among men, and which is a partial act, the choice of the hands, of the eyes, of the appetites, and not a whole act of the man. But that which I call right or goodness is the choice of my constitution; and that which I call heaven, and inwardly aspire after, is the state or circumstance desirable to my constitution; and the action which I in all my years tend to do, is the work for my faculties. We must hold a man amenable to reason for the choice of his daily craft or profession. It is not an excuse any longer for his deeds, that they are the custom of his trade. What business has he with an evil trade? Has he not a calling in his character.

Each man has his own vocation. The talent is the call. There is one direction in which all space is open to him. He has faculties silently inviting him thither to endless exertion. He is like a ship in a river; he runs against obstructions on every side but one; on that side all obstruction is taken away, and he sweeps serenely over a deepening channel into an infinite sea. This talent and this call depend on his organization, or the mode in which the general soul incarnates itself in him. He inclines to do something which is easy to him, and good when it is done, but which no other man can do. He has no rival. For the more truly he consults his own powers, the more difference will his work exhibit from the work of any other. His ambition is exactly proportioned to his powers. The height of the pinnacle is determined by the breadth of the base. Every man has this call of the power to do somewhat unique, and no man has any other call. The pretense that he has another call, a summons by name and personal election and outward "signs that mark him extraordinary, and not in the roll of common men," is fanaticism, and betrays obtuseness to perceive that there is one mind in all the individuals, and no respect of persons therein.

By doing his work, he makes the need felt which he can supply, and creates the taste by which he is enjoyed. By doing his own work, he unfolds himself. It is the vice of our public speaking that it has not abandonment. Somewhere, not only every orator but every man should let out all the length of all the reins; should find or make a frank and hearty expression of what force and meaning is in him. The common experience is, that the man fits himself as well as he can to the customary details of that work or trade he falls into, and tends it as a dog turns a spit. Then is he a part of the machine he moves; the man is lost. Until he can manage to communicate himself to others in his full stature and proportion, he does not yet find his vocation. He must find in that an outlet for his character, so that he may justify his work to their eyes. If the labor is mean, let him by his thinking and character make it liberal. Whatever he knows and thinks, whatever in his apprehension is worth doing, that let him communicate, or men will never know and honor him aright. Foolish, whenever you take the meanness and formality of that thing you do, instead of converting it into the obedient spiracle of your character and aims.

# Appendix II—
# Passages on the Examined Life:
# Emerson and the Examined Life

T HESE excerpts from Emerson's works, including his private journals, reflect his interest in and concern for self-recovery and are offered here as a convenience for readers who may wish to have a series of entries for further study. They were assembled by the author and read in Faneuil Hall, Boston, by Poet Laureate Robert Pinsky on June 28, 2003, as part of the Emerson Bicentennial celebrations. Those readers who wish to watch and listen to Mr. Pinsky's reading can find it at http://forum-network.org/lecture/emerson-and-examined-life.

from *Experience*

It is very unhappy, but too late to be helped, the discovery we have made, that we exist. That discovery is called the Fall of Man. Ever afterwards, we suspect our instruments. We have learned that we do not see directly, that we have no means of correcting these colored and distorting lenses which we are, or of computing the amount of their errors. Perhaps these subject-lenses have a creative power; perhaps there are no objects. Once we lived in what we saw; now, the rapaciousness of this new power, which threatens to absorb all things, engages us.

from *The Over-Soul*

Man is a stream whose source is hidden. Our being is descending into us from we know not whence. I am constrained every moment to acknowledge a higher origin for events than the will I call mine.

There is a difference between one and another hour of life, in their authority and subsequent effect. Our faith comes in moments; our vice is habitual. Yet there is a depth in those brief moments which constrains us to ascribe more reality to them than to all other experiences. . . .

We live in succession, in division, in parts, in particles. Meantime within man is the soul of the whole; the wise silence; the universal beauty, to which every part and particle is equally related; the eternal One. And this deep power in which we exist, and whose beatitude is all accessible to us, is not only self-sufficing and perfect in every hour, but the act of seeing and the thing seen, the seer and the spectacle, the subject and the object, are one.

from *Experience*

Where [then] do we find ourselves? In a series of which we do not know the extremes, and believe that it has none. We wake and find ourselves on a stair; there are stairs below us, which we seem to have ascended; there are stairs above us, many a one, which go upward and out of sight. But the Genius which, according to the old belief, stands at the door by which we enter, and gives us the lethe to drink, that we may tell no tales, mixed the cup too strongly, and we cannot shake off the lethargy now at noonday. Sleep lingers all our lifetime about our eyes, as night hovers all day in the boughs of the fir-tree. All things swim and glitter. Our life is not so much threatened as our perception. Ghostlike we glide through nature, and should not know our place again.

We live amid surfaces, and the true art of life is to skate well on them. . . . Life itself is a mixture of power and form, and will not bear the least excess of either. To finish the moment, to find the journey's end in every step of the road, to live the greatest number of good hours, is wisdom.

*from Senses and the Soul*

And yet there seems no need to fear that we should grow too wise. The path of truth has obstacles enough of its own. We dwell on the surface of nature. We dwell amidst surfaces; and surface laps so closely on surface, that we cannot easily pierce to see the interior organism. Then the subtlety of things! Under every cause, another cause. Truth soars too high or dives too deep, for the most resolute inquirer. See of how much we know nothing.

Our ignorance is great enough, and yet the fact most surprising is not our ignorance, but the aversion of men from knowledge. That which, one would say, would unite all minds and join all hands, the ambition to push as far as fate would permit, the planted garden of man on every hand into the kingdom of Night, really fires the heart of few and solitary men. Tell men to study themselves, and for the most part, they find nothing less interesting.

*from Self-Reliance*

That popular fable of the sot who was picked up dead drunk in the street, carried to the duke's house, washed and dressed and laid in the duke's bed, and, on his waking, treated with all obsequious ceremony like the duke, and assured that he had been insane, owes its popularity to the fact, that it symbolizes so well the state of man, who is in the world a sort of sot, but now and then wakes up, exercises his reason, and finds himself a true prince.

We lie in the lap of immense intelligence, which makes us receivers of its truth and organs of its activity. When we discern justice, when we discern truth, we do nothing of ourselves, but allow a passage to its beams. If we ask whence this comes, if we seek to pry into the soul that causes, all philosophy is at fault. Its presence or its absence is all we can affirm. Every man discriminates between the voluntary acts of his mind, and his involuntary perceptions, and knows that to his involuntary perceptions a perfect faith is due. He may err in the expression of them, but he knows that these things are so, like day and night, not to be disputed.

Nothing is at last sacred but the integrity of your own mind. Absolve you to yourself, and you shall have the suffrage of the world. I remember an answer which when quite young I was prompted to make to a valued adviser, who was wont to importune me with the dear old doctrines of the church. On my saying, What have I to do with the sacredness of traditions, if I live wholly from within? my friend suggested, —"But these impulses may be from below, not from above." I replied, "They do not seem to me to be such; but if I am the Devil's child, I will live then from the Devil." No law can be sacred to me but that of my nature.

In this pleasing, contrite wood-life which God allows me, let me record day by day my honest thought without prospect or retrospect, and, I cannot doubt, it will be found symmetrical, though I mean it not, and see it not. My book should smell of pines and resound with the hum of insects. The swallow over my window should interweave that thread or straw he carries in his bill into my web also. . . .
For, the sense of being which in calm hours rises, we know not how, in the soul, is not diverse from things, from space, from light, from time, from man, but one with them, and proceeds obviously from the same source whence their life and being also proceed. . . .

And now at last the highest truth on this subject remains unsaid; probably cannot be said; for all that we say is the far-off remembering of the intuition. That thought, by what I can now nearest approach to say it, is this: When good is near you, when you have life in yourself, it is not by any known or accustomed way; you shall not discern the foot-prints of any other; you shall not see the face of man; you shall not hear any name; —the way, the thought, the good, shall be wholly strange and new. . . .

I must be myself. I cannot break myself any longer for you, or you. If you can love me for what I am, we shall be the happier. If you cannot, I will still seek to deserve that you should. I will not hide my tastes or aversions. I will so trust that what is deep is holy, that I will do strongly before the sun and moon whatever inly rejoices me, and the heart appoints. If you are noble, I will love you; if you are not, I will not hurt you and myself by hypocritical attentions. If you are true, but not in the same truth with me, cleave to your companions; I will seek my own. . . .

I do this not selfishly, but humbly and truly. It is alike your interest, and mine, and all men's, however long we have dwelt in lies, to live in truth. Does this sound harsh today? You will soon love what is dictated by your nature as well as mine, and, if we follow the truth, it will bring us out safe at last. But so you may give these friends pain. Yes, but I cannot sell my liberty and my power, to save their sensibility. Besides, all persons have their moments of reason, when they look out into the region of absolute truth; then will they justify me, and do the same thing.

from *Journal, 1840*

In all my lectures, I have taught one doctrine, namely, the infinitude of the private man. This the people accept readily enough, and even with loud commendation, as long as I call the lecture Art, or Politics, of Literature, or the Household; but the moment I call it Religion, they are shocked, though it be only the application of the same truth which they receive everywhere else, to a new class of facts. . . .

from *Divinity School Address*

Meantime, whilst the doors of the temple stand open, night and day, before every man, and the oracles of this truth cease never, it is guarded by one stern condition; this, namely; it is an intuition. It cannot be received at second hand. Truly speaking, it is not instruction, but provocation, that I can receive from another soul. What he announces, I must find true in me, or wholly reject; and on his word, or as his second, be he who he may, I can accept nothing. On the contrary, the absence of this primary faith is the presence of degradation. As is the flood so is the ebb. Let this faith depart, and the very words it spake, and the

things it made, become false and hurtful. Then falls the church, the
state, art, letters, life. The doctrine of the divine nature being forgotten,
a sickness infects and dwarfs the constitution. Once man was all; now he
is an appendage, a nuisance. And because the indwelling Supreme Spirit
cannot wholly be got rid of, the doctrine of it suffers this perversion,
that the divine nature is attributed to one or two persons, and denied
to all the rest, and denied with fury.

Jesus Christ belonged to the true race of prophets. He saw with open
eye the mystery of the soul. Drawn by its severe harmony, ravished with
its beauty, he lived in it, and had his being there. Alone in all history,
he estimated the greatness of man. One man was true to what is in you
and me. He saw that God incarnates himself in man, and evermore
goes forth anew to take possession of his world. He said, in this jubilee
of sublime emotion, 'I am divine. Through me, God acts; through me,
speaks. Would you see God, see me; or, see thee, when thou also thinkest
as I now think.' But what a distortion did his doctrine and memory suffer
in the same, in the next, and the following ages! There is no doctrine
of the Reason which will bear to be taught by the Understanding. The
understanding caught this high chant from the poet's lips, and said, in
the next age, 'This was Jehovah come down out of heaven. I will kill
you, if you say he was a man.' . . .

It is time that this ill-suppressed murmur of all thoughtful men
against the famine of our churches; this moaning of the heart because it
is bereaved of the consolation, the hope, the grandeur, that come alone
out of the culture of the moral nature; should be heard through the sleep
of indolence, and over the din of routine . . . The test of the true faith,
certainly, should be its power to charm and command the soul, as the
laws of nature control the activity of the hands, —so commanding that
we find pleasure and honor in obeying. The faith should blend with the
light of rising and of setting suns, with the flying cloud, the singing bird,
and the breath of flowers.

from *The Over-Soul*

The soul is the perceiver and revealer of truth. We know truth when we see it, let skeptic and scoffer say what they choose. Foolish people ask you, when you have spoken what they do not wish to hear, 'How do you know it is truth, and not an error of your own?' We know truth when we see it, from opinion, as we know when we are awake that we are awake. We distinguish the announcements of the soul, its manifestations of its own nature, by the term "Revelation." These are always attended by the emotion of the sublime. For this communication is an influx of the Divine mind into our mind.

The nature of these revelations is the same; they are perceptions of the absolute law. They are solutions of the soul's own questions. They do not answer the questions which the understanding asks. The soul answers never by words, but by the thing itself that is inquired after.

This energy does not descend into individual life on any other condition than entire possession. It comes to the lowly and simple; it comes to whomsoever will put off what is foreign and proud; it comes as insight; it comes as serenity and grandeur. When we see those whom it inhabits, we are apprized of new degrees of greatness.

Let man, then, learn the revelation of all nature and all thought to his heart; this, namely; that the Highest dwells with him; that the sources of nature are in his own mind, if the sentiment of duty is there. But if he would know what the great God speaketh, he must 'go into his closet and shut the door,' as Jesus said. God will not make himself manifest to cowards. He must greatly listen to himself, withdrawing himself from all the accents of other men's devotion.

from *Nature*, "Prospects"

I shall therefore conclude this essay with some traditions of man and nature, which a certain poet sang to me; and which, as they have always been in the world, and perhaps reappear to every bard, may be both history and prophecy. . . .

'The foundations of man are not in matter, but in spirit. But the element of spirit is eternity. To it, therefore, the longest series of events, the oldest chronologies are young and recent. In the cycle of the universal man, from whom the known individuals proceed, centuries are points, and all history is but the epoch of one degradation.

'We distrust and deny inwardly our sympathy with nature. We own and disown our relation to it, by turns. We are, like Nebuchadnezzar, dethroned, bereft of reason, and eating grass like an ox. But who can set limits to the remedial force of spirit?

'A man is a god in ruins. When men are innocent, life shall be longer, and shall pass into the immortal, as gently as we awake from dreams. Now, the world would be insane and rabid, if these disorganizations should last for hundreds of years. It is kept in check by death and infancy. Infancy is the perpetual Messiah, which comes into the arms of fallen men, and pleads with them to return to paradise.

'Man is the dwarf of himself. Once he was permeated and dissolved by spirit. He filled nature with his overflowing currents. But, having made for himself this huge shell, his waters retired; he no longer fills the veins and veinlets; he is shrunk to a drop. He sees, that the structure still fits him, but fits him colossally. Say, rather, once it fitted him, now it corresponds to him from far and on high. He adores timidly his own work. Yet sometimes he starts in his slumber, and wonders at himself and his house, and muses strangely at the resemblance betwixt him and it. He perceives that if his law is still paramount, if still he have elemental power, if his word is sterling yet in nature, it is not conscious power, it is not inferior but superior to his will. It is Instinct.' Thus my Orphic poet sang.

from *Experience*

I know that the world I converse with in the city and in the farms, is not the world I think. I observe that difference and shall observe it. One day, I shall know the value and law of this discrepance. But I have not found that much was gained by manipular attempts to realize the world of thought. Many eager persons successively make an experiment in this way, and make themselves ridiculous. . . .

But far be from me the despair which prejudges the law by a paltry empiricism, —since there never was a right endeavor, but it succeeded. Patience and patience, we shall win at the last. We must be very suspicious of the deceptions of the element of time. It takes a good deal of time to eat or to sleep, or to earn a hundred dollars, and a very little time to entertain a hope and an insight which becomes the light of our life. We dress our garden, eat our dinners, discuss the household with our wives, and these things make no impression, are forgotten next week; but in the solitude to which every man is always returning, he has a sanity and revelations, which in his passage into new worlds he will carry with him. Never mind the ridicule, never mind the defeat: up again, old heart! —it seems to say, —there is victory yet for all justice; and the true romance which the world exists to realize, will be the transformation of genius into practical power.

from "*Tragedy*"

All that life demands of us through the greater part of the day is an equilibrium, a readiness, open eyes and ears, and free hands. Society asks this, and truth, and love, and the genius of our life.

# Notes

## Preface

10    Though a great poet . . . : Charles Ives, *Essays Before a Sonata* (W.W. Norton & Co., New York, 1961), 11.

## Introduction

12    This is a most happy . . . : Stanley Cavell, *Conditions Handsome and Unhandsome* (U. of Chicago Press, 1990), 129.

14    Emerson lingered . . . : Robert Richardson, *Emerson: The Mind on Fire* (U. of California Press, Berkeley, 1995), 565.

15    the infinitude of the private man . . . : Ralph Waldo Emerson, *The Journals and Miscellaneous Notebooks*, vol. VII (Harvard U. Press, Cambridge, 1969), 342.

## Chapter 1: Our Secret Melancholy

17    a secret melancholy . . . : Ralph Waldo Emerson, "New England Reformers," *Essays II*.

18    I speak of the relation . . . : Lionel Trilling, *The Opposing Self* (Harcourt Brace Jovanovitch, New York, 1955), ii.

23    The soul lets no man go . . .: Ralph Waldo Emerson, "New England Reformers," *Essays II.*

## Chapter 2: Deeper Prisons

24    I visited the prison . . .: Ralph Waldo Emerson, *The Journals and Miscellaneous Notebooks,* vol. III, (Harvard U. Press, Cambridge, 1969), 100.

28    what a man is thinking . . .: Ralph Waldo Emerson, "Natural History of the Intellect," Volume XII.

29    We are reminded again . . . Ralph Waldo Emerson, "Spiritual Laws," *Essays I.*

## Chapter 3: Emerson and American Religion

33    was in his conviction . . .: Robert Richardson, *Emerson: The Mind on Fire* (U. of California Press, Berkeley, 1995), 292.

34    Spiritual Idealism See *The Essential Transcendentalists,* Tarcher/Penguin, 2005.

37    every desire of the human . . .: *Complete Sermons of Ralph Waldo Emerson,* vol. 1., ed. Albert J. Von Frank (U. of Missouri Press, Columbia, 1989), 57.

43    Caldwell quotes . . .: Christopher Caldwell, *Reflections on the Revolution in Europe* (Doubleday, 2009).

43    whenever we live rightly . . .: Ralph Waldo Emerson, *The Journals and Miscellaneous Notebooks*, vol. IV, 313.

## Chapter 5: Idealism and the Perennial Philosophy

54    Self-culture is the thought . . .: Those involved in so-called spiritual work make a sharp distinction between the spiritual and the religious, whereas in the general culture these two terms are most often interchangeable. In Emerson's case, "spiritual" refers to an

element in existence as opposed to a "material" element. He said in *Nature,* "The presence of a higher, namely, of the spiritual element is essential to [nature's] perfection."

54   the Perennial Philosophy .... "The Tradition" ...: William W. Quinn, *The Only Tradition* (State U. of New York Press, 1997).

54   Advaita Vedanta ...: Swami Paramananda, *Emerson and Vedanta* (The Vedanta Center, Boston, 1918).

60   The weakness of the scientific position ...: William W. Quinn, *The Only Tradition* (State U. of New York Press, 1997), 317.

62   the Latin word *virtu* ...: Thomas Moore, *The Planets Within* (Lindisfarne Press, 1990), 32.

## Chapter 6: The Perennial Philosophy Applied

64   "transparent eye-ball revelation" ...: This experience, from chapter 1 of *Nature,* is the only true mystical experience recorded by Emerson in his public works. It reads as follows: "Crossing a bare common, in snow puddles, at twilight, under a clouded sky, without having in my thoughts any occurrence of special good fortune, I have enjoyed a perfect exhilaration. I am glad to the brink of fear. In the woods too, a man casts off his years, as the snake his slough, and at what period soever of life, is always a child. In the woods, is perpetual youth. Within these plantations of God, a decorum and sanctity reign, a perennial festival is dressed, and the guest sees not how he should tire of them in a thousand years. In the woods, we return to reason and faith. There I feel that nothing can befall me in life, —no disgrace, no calamity, (leaving me my eyes,) which nature cannot repair. Standing on the bare ground, —my head bathed by the blithe air, and uplifted into infinite space, —all mean egotism vanishes. I become a transparent eye-ball; I am nothing; I see all; the currents of the Universal Being circulate through me; I am part or particle of God."

67     attractive and repellent way . . .: Stanley Cavell, *Emerson's Transcendental Etudes*, (Stanford U. Press, Palo Alto, 2003), 188.

67     I feel like God . . .: Stephen Mansfield, *The Faith of George W. Bush* (Tarcher/Penguin, New York, 2003).

74     Every truth is a . . .: Ralph Waldo Emerson, *The Journals and Miscellaneous Notebooks*, vol. IV, 381.

75     I am always insincere . . .: Ralph Waldo Emerson, "Nominalist and Realist," *Essays II.*

## Chapter 7: Modern Physics and Theories of Consciousness

78     Out of my experience . . .: William James, 1909, quoted in F.O. Mattheissen, *The James Family* (Alfred A. Knopf, New York, 1947), 588–89.

81     rumors of space/time's . . .: Brian Greene, *The Fabric of the Cosmos* (Alfred A. Knopf, New York, 2004), 472.

81     Any universe . . .: Roger Penrose, *The Road to Reality* (Jonathan Cape, London, 2004), 1030.

82     must be a real physical process . . .: ibid, 1032.

84     The more the universe . . .: Amit Goswami, *The Self-Aware Universe* (Tarcher/Penguin, New York, 1995), 130.

84     What is life but . . .: Ralph Waldo Emerson, *The Journals and Miscellaneous Notebooks*, vol. X, 146.

89     the legend is tossed . . .: Ralph Waldo Emerson, "Quotation and Originality," *Letters and Social Aims.*

91     seven major gods of the Vedic tradition. . .: One possible list: Brahma, Varuna, Surya, Agni, Soma, Rudra, and Yama. However, there are many lists. Brahma eventually replaced the old gods as the one true God of the Vedas.

92     There is no other world . . .: Robert Richardson, *Emerson: The Mind on Fire* (U. of California Press, Berkeley, 1995), 382.

## Chapter 8: The Condition of Sanity

109   Emerson in later years . . .: By the 1850s, Emerson was ranked as one of the richest men in Massachusetts, having had his finances organized and overseen by William Forbes, who married Emerson's second daughter Edith.

109   We like very well . . .: Ralph Waldo Emerson, "Considerations by the Way," *Conduct of Life.*

## Chapter 9: A Call to the Nation

111   The essay "Fate" . . .: Stanley Cavell, *Emerson's Transcendental Etudes,* (Stanford U. Press, Palo Alto, 2003), 194.

112   Dean Hamer's assertion . . .: Dean Hamer, *The God Gene* (Anchor Books, New York, 2005).

113   Nothing befalls us . . .: Ralph Waldo Emerson, "Fate," *The Later Lectures,* Volume I, 257.

113   A long storm . . .: Ralph Waldo Emerson, *The Journals and Miscellaneous Notebooks,* vol. III, 102.

113   within sight of land . . .: Robert Richardson, *Emerson: The Mind on Fire* (U. of California Press, Berkeley, 1995), 483.

114   Grey clouds . . .: Ralph Waldo Emerson, *The Later Lectures,* Volume I, 249.

## Chapter 10: A New Great Awakening

134   The curse of our present times . . .: Henry James, Sr., quoted in Philip Gura, *American Transcendentalism* (Hill and Wang, New York, 2007), 216.

## Chapter 11: Wealth and Economy

138   According to the Federal Reserve . . .: On average, today's consumer has a total of fourteen credit obligations on record at a credit

bureau. These include credit cards (such as department store charge cards, gas cards, or bank cards) and installment loans (auto loans, mortgage loans, student loans, etc.). Not included are savings and checking accounts (typically not reported to a credit bureau). Of these fourteen credit obligations, ten are likely to be credit cards and four are likely to be installment loans. (Source: FICO, Jan., 2008) $84,454 is the average household's personal debt, including mortgages, cars loans, credit cards, and other personal debt. (Source: *USA Today,* Oct. 4, 2004)

However, if one looks at the statistics gathered by reputable organizations, such as the Federal Reserve Board, the myth that the majority of Americans are over their heads in debt is simply not true. Contrary to popular belief, a little more than half, or about 56 percent of Americans, do not carry much debt at all and typically pay off their credit card balances in full each month. Only a very small percentage of the remaining 44 percent of Americans carry too much debt. The truth is that only a tiny percentage of Americans have too much debt.

# Index of Names

RICHARD G. GELDARD is a full-time writer and lecturer living in New York City and the Hudson Valley. He is married to the artist and writer Astrid Fitzgerald. Before retiring to write full time, he taught Greek Philosophy and The Science of Mind at Yeshiva College in New York. He is a graduate of Bowdoin College and Stanford University, where he earned his doctorate in Dramatic Literature and Classics. A frequent lecturer, he was a featured speaker at Faneuil Hall in Boston as part of the Emerson Bicentennial Celebrations in 2003, and in June, 2005, he delivered the keynote at the re-instatement of the Delphic Games in Delphi, Greece. In June 2011, he will speak on Neoplatonism at the new library in Alexandria, Egypt.